An Introduction to Trail and Fell Running

By

Keven Shevels

publications

First published in Great Britain in 2006 by Trailguides Limited.
Second edition published in Great Britain in 2010 by Trailguides Limited.
www.trailguides.co.uk

ISBN 978-1-905444-40-3

Trailguides Limited
35 Carmel Road South
Darlington
Co Durham DL3 8DQ

Cover design by Steve Gustard.

Contents

Contents continued.

1. Introduction

Trail and fell running. It conjures up pictures of the lone runner striding majestically across the open countryside. And believe me, it can be just like the picture that you've imagined.

Over recent years the number of runners competing in trail and fell races has grown considerably as has the number of races around the country. For the runner trying trail and fell for the first time it can be a little daunting lining up at the start of your first race not really knowing what you have let yourself in for.

This is where this training guide comes in. Its purpose is to lay bare all those little details and prepare the first timer and the not so experienced for what can be the most pleasurable running activity in existence.

We will explain the different types of runs and races that make up trail and fell running, preparation for the race, the technical aspects of this type of running and what to expect at, during and after the event.

"The Dream"

2. What is Trail and Fell Running.

Very good question, so lets begin with the toughies first.

The British Athletics Federation laid down the definitive and accurate but extremely boring definition of trail running events in 1995. The British Athletics Federation being the forerunner of today's UK Athletics.

"In the context of athletics, trail races are primarily along footpaths and bridlepaths marked on Ordnance Survey maps as "public rights of way". They are "highways" to which pedestrians have unrestricted access in English law. Towpaths, forest drives, farm cart tracks and paths in parks etc, from which motorised traffic is excluded, are also trails when the owners' permission is obtained."

Both fell running and trail running fit into this definition. So what are the differences and what are the similarities between the two.

Where the real difference between the two springs up is in the nature of the terrain the runner travels over. Trail running events are held throughout the UK and can cover a whole variety of terrain ranging from lowland rural areas, canal towpaths, disused railway lines to forests, moors and even mountain routes. As a result the running surface that you are travelling over can vary enormously and a particular run may even have several types of surface underfoot such as grass, gravel, earth, stone etc.

> Running on surfaces other than tarmac is commonly called "off-road" running. This is a catch-all description and does not really differentiate between the two types, trail and fell.

On the other hand fell running is staged in areas that are exclusively classed as fell, hill or mountain terrain, basically the upland areas. As with trail races the running surface may be any combination of grass, gravel, earth, etc although they can also include significant stretches of rougher terrain such as heather beds, boulder fields and peat bog.

The most significant difference between the two is the amount of climbing and descending. In a fell race, this tends to be more extreme than in a corresponding trail race. However the milder fell runs and the tougher trail runs do sometimes overlap and it could be difficult to decide where a particular race would lie. This results in some events registered as fell runs that could be described as trail runs and vice versa.

As a generalisation, be prepared to do more walking in a fell race than a trail race as the type of terrain can limit the amount of running, and the climbing can be steeper and longer.

Whether it is the high moors of the Pennines (front cover and below) or the mountains of the Lakes, fell running can let you explore some of the most scenic wild places in the country.

Whereas trail can take you from forest, to field, to river (back cover), to disused railway track. In fact you name a surface and there will be a race on it.

As for distance, both trail and fell runs can be any length. Many ultra-races (distances greater than the marathon) are trail events but so are many shorter races with the shortest starting at about two miles. Again, there is no set distance so you have the freedom to run as far and for as long as you want.

Below, a table has been set out in order to categorise the differences between trail, fell and mountain runs. The table provides an assessment of the type of country that the route would be travelling over plus an indication of the type of factors that would need to be considered for tackling the route. It has broken down the types of country into three categories, namely Trail, Fell and Mountain. Assessing which category best fits the route gives the indicator as whether a route could be classed as trail, fell or mountain. Be aware that a particular route may not necessarily fit into a certain category exactly. In this situation, it would be a case of best fit.

2.1 Why run off-road ?

I first started running nearly thirty years ago when the "running boom" took off. At that time everything was road runs with half-marathons and marathons kicking up all over the place. Being a young and tender "sprog" in my early twenties I very quickly got into the spirit of the thing and the competition and it

wasn't long before I was competing virtually every weekend. Although with hindsight and from the safety of an expanding waistline, I have to admit that the ratio of enthusiasm to talent was very heavily stacked to the enthusiasm side of the scale.

After a couple of years pounding the tarmac I tried my first fell race. Bing ! Flashing Lights ! The Full Conversion Job !!!

Before the race was even

Both trail and fell running can be a year round activity. With the correct shoes to provide grip and suitable clothing virtually all weather conditions can be coped with.

	TRAIL	FELL	MOUNTAIN
Description	Lowland and forest areas including urban, cultivated and forested locations	Moorlands and upland areas which may include some upland cultivated and forestry areas plus possibly remote locations	Upland and mountain areas including remote and isolated locations
Height	Not usually above 1,000 feet but may go up to 2,500 feet	Usually above 1,000 feet, up to 2,500 feet and above.	Usually above 2,500 feet and up to 4,000 feet
Way-marking	Usually	Limited	None
Terrain	Usually graded paths, tracks and trails but may include some off-trail	May include some graded paths, tracks and trails but mainly off-trail	Virtually all off-trail
Height gain	Limited height gain	May include considerable height gain	May include some severe height gain
Effects of weather	Very limited effect	May be prone to sudden weather changes	Extreme weather a possibility
Navigational skills	None to basic	Basic to competent	Competent to expert
Equipment	Running - Trail shoes Possibly waterproofs Food and drink dependant upon route	Running - Trail/fell shoes Full waterproof cover. Possibly map and compass dependant upon route. Food and drink dependant upon route	Running - Fell shoes Full waterproof cover Map and compass Food and drink
Escape Routes	Yes	Some	Some to nil

Notes: Graded paths = Well established paths with a stable surface. Escape routes = The opportunity to cut the route short and return to the start without completing the full course in the event of weather changes or unforeseen incidents.

finished I knew that this is what running was all about. Stuff the tarmac, running off-road was where the soul was. Let slip the shackles and let it run as free as I was moving over the open country.

In those days trail running wasn't even a gleam in anybody's eye. There was cross-country, road or fell. Oh and there were even some fancy prima-donnas doing something called track. Naturally I gravitated towards the fell running and served quite an enthralling apprenticeship working my way through the fell runner's calendar. Then gradually, one by one, a few trail races started to appear and so I tried one or two. Bing ! The same feeling was there and so I became hooked on trail running as well as fell running.

One of the beauties of running off-road is that it can stimulate the mind as well. Unlike road running where you can get into a rhythm and blot-out the mind as you plod around, off-road running requires a higher degree of concentration, thinking and decision-making as you run. This is caused by the requirements of foot placement, constantly changing running style and the need to always be aware of where you are to avoid running off-course. If your event requires navigation and decisions about route choice, then this cerebral element is even more enhanced.

Then it slowly dawned on me, there was no real difference between the two. Other than the severity of the terrain, they were one and the same. Just being out there in the country, away from tarmac and crowds and traffic.

And the sights I've seen. An early morning run by the river Tees being interrupted by watching an aerial dogfight between two herons arguing over territory. A barn owl flying silently alongside me as if the pair of us were together while on an evening run. The white backsides of deer disappearing into the undergrowth as you pass. And there's many more moments like that stored in the old brain cells.

If you can think of any better reasons for not running off-road, then let me know.

2.2 Governing bodies:

There is no one overall governing body for off-road running in the UK. Instead it has developed over time on a sort of patchwork basis with the two distinct branches of trail running and fell running having their own separate governing bodies.

Fell running is the older of the two branches and has traditions going back over a hundred years with local show races. Within England fell running is governed by the Fell Runner's Association (FRA). This body is a constituent body of UK Athletics and governs fell running in England on it's behalf. The FRA grants permits for fell running events and manages the rules for competition for fell races. All fell races within England must be registered with the FRA.

Individuals may join the FRA as members. For the annual subscription you receive a fixtures calendar each year listing all fell races in England and also some in Scotland and Wales. There is also a members magazine which is published on a four-monthly basis which contains results, news and articles that are of interest to the fell runner. In Northern Ireland, Scotland and Wales the situation is slightly different. Although not governing bodies, the following organisations represent the interests of fell runners in their respective areas and are open for individual members to join. The benefits of joining are very similar to those listed above for the FRA and apart from the governing body status for any mention of the FRA you can substitute the relevant association.

The Northern Ireland Mountain Runners Association
The Scottish Hill Runners Association
The Welsh Fell Runners Association.

If you are serious about fell running then it is worth considering joining the relevant association. Further information can be found on the websites at
www.fellrunner.org.uk
www.nimra.org.uk
www.shr.uk.com
www.wfra.org.uk

Similar to the FRA is the Trail Runner's Association (TRA), which again, governs the sport of trail running on behalf of UK Athletics.

The TRA issues permits for trail races and manages the national championship. The TRA is stronger in the south of the country than the north but is rapidly gaining popularity "up country". It is worth noting that in certain parts of the country trail races may be registered with the local county athletics association. In which case they tend to be classed as a multi-terrain race rather than a trail race.

As with the FRA, individual runners may join the TRA with similar benefits of a fixture calendar and a member's newsletter.

For further information see the TRA website at
www.tra-uk.org

In addition to these two bodies there also exists the Long Distance Walker's Association (LDWA). As its name suggests this is an association of walkers that favour long distance challenges. Where this comes of interest to the runner is that the vast majority of these events welcome runners. It's members organise events of 20 miles and over, some upto 50 or 60 miles in length and for the more extreme, there is also the annual LDWA 100 mile event which is held in a different part of the country every year. The LDWA events are very well organised and have a good friendly atmosphere and are great fun to participate in. With events in all parts of the country these challenge walks cover trail, fell and even mountain terrain. Because of the long distances of these events, some of them can cover all three types of terrain in the one event.

The LDWA is not a part of UK Athletics and so, while some LDWA organisers do register their events with one of the UK Athletics governing bodies, most don't. This means that these events are technically not registered athletic events. Whilst you can enter and compete as an individual, UK Athletics rules forbid you to enter as a club member and wear your club vest.

As with both the FRA and the TRA, the individual runner can join the LDWA. Again there are similar benefits with a list of fixtures and a member's news magazine. For further information see the LDWA website at **www.ldwa.org.uk**

2.3 Clubs:

As with all branches of athletics there are clubs that cater for those who love off-road running. These clubs may be "general" athletics clubs catering for all branches of athletics or they may be specialist clubs that only cater for off-road running.

The "general" clubs may have a number of members who enjoy running off-road be it trail or fell. In some of them they form specialist sections in the same way that you would have a road running section or a track and field section.

In the more traditional fell running areas of the country such as the north of England and parts of Scotland and Wales, there are clubs that are purely specialist fell running clubs. These clubs do not register for or partake in any of the other athletic disciplines. Members of these clubs may also belong to second clubs for whom they compete on the road, cross-country or track and field.

Some of the web sites of the governing bodies have links to the websites of those clubs that participate in their discipline. It is worth looking up and seeing if there is a local club that does cater for you.

2.4 Types of events:

This section gives a brief summery of the nature of the different types of off-road events so that you can familiarise yourself with what to expect.

Short Fell Races

Under six miles. With most of these events the course will consist of running to the top of a hill, fell or mountain and then running back to the finish. The route will invariably be an out and back course or a loop course with the summit at somewhere around the mid-point. There will normally only be the one major climb on these events leading up to the summit. This means that the course will probably be split 50/50 uphill and downhill. The terrain can be anything from graded track, to tussocky grass, to rocky paths, and there may be significant climbing. These routes are sometimes marked but again there are significant numbers of them that aren't.

Short distance Trail Races

Under thirteen miles. Runs in rural terrain normally on public rights of way such as footpaths or bridleways or on permissive rights of way (with the owners permission) over private land. A large number of events are held on Forestry Commission land. Courses are normally marked and the navigational ability required is limited to ensuring that you do not stray off-route. The climbing on these courses will be dependent upon the part of the country the event is in and may range from being flat, such as along a canal towpath, to being quite hilly. Even the hilly trail courses will not be as severe as the average fell course although there may be an overlap between tough trail courses and the mild fell race courses. The terrain involved is normally graded path or track, field paths or, normally at the worst, rough pasture. However some events do sometimes "toughen up" particular sections to make them more of a challenge.

Medium Fell Races

Over six miles but under twelve. Not normally out and back courses but you do get the rare exception. The courses are usually some form of a loop. Often several major climbs on the route although on those races that do go up major mountains such as the Ben Nevis or Snowdon races there is just the one very big one. As a result the routes can be any proportion of up, down and level running. The terrain can be anything from graded track, to tussocky grass, to rocky paths, and there may be significant climbing. These routes are often marked but again there are significant numbers of them that aren't.

Middle Distance Trail Races

Over thirteen miles but under thirty miles. Runs in rural terrain as with short distance trail races. The terrain is also similar to the short distance runs. Although in certain parts of the country may include moorland paths and tracks. Due to the distances involved courses are not normally marked but they are held on public rights of way and where the course follows a particular route such as the High Peak Trail then that route's own particular way markers would provide an aid to navigation. Some events may be both TRA middle distance trail races and LDWA events with both runners and walkers partaking.

Long Fell Races
Over twelve miles. Distances can range from twelve miles to thirty, in some cases more. Can involve long completion times. Will involve visiting several major summits with a considerable amount of climbing. Routes rarely marked and will require a degree of navigational ability. These courses normally contain a high proportion of rough moorland/fell /mountain terrain. Should not be attempted by those runners who have no experience of travelling in this type of country.

Ultra Distance Trail Races
Over thirty miles in distance. Some may be of considerable distance such as the Grand Union Canal Race at 145 miles. Run in rural terrain the same as short and middle distance events. Due to the distances involved these are not normally suitable for the beginner to trail running. For more information on these type of challenge events see our sister publication "Long and Ultra distance Off-Road Running".

LDWA Events
Primarily walker's events or challenge walks. A majority of them are open to runners but not all. Although open to runners, some of these events are non-competitive and do not give prizes or issue results. However some do and it is worth checking the entry form if being on the prize list is important to you. The events can be any distance from twenty miles upwards. They are held throughout the country so the terrain can quite literally be anything that the British countryside holds. The same applies to the amount of climbing involved, it can range from a couple of feet to a couple of thousand feet. These events are rarely marked and require a degree of navigational competence. Some of these events may also be registered as trail or fell races.

Mountain Marathons
Primarily two day events although there are a number of one day and even three day events in the country. They are held in wild remote mountainous areas for teams of two. They are a two day navigation exercise with the competitors finding their way round a series of checkpoints known as controls. All food, drink and equipment required for the two days has to be carried by the competitors. These are very challenging events both physically and mentally and are wholly enjoyable as can be seen by the fact that most of the events are full before the closing date. If the thought of doing one of these monsters appeals to you then more information on equipment and training can be found in our sister publication "Mountain Marathon Preparation".

Orienteering

A specialist form of off-road running that involves navigating your way round a laid-out course. Basically it is a competitive navigation exercise. Highly recommended for fun and enjoyment and also brushing up on your navigation skills. Orienteering courses are contained within a relatively small area by endurance running standards, so the chances of getting completely lost are minimal. There are a range of different colour-coded courses at these events to suit different fitness and navigation levels. Orienteering is outside the scope of this book but more information can be found on the British Orienteering Association's website at www.britishorienteering.org.uk

3. Preparing for a Trail or Fell Run.

Many people run in the country purely for training purposes and enjoyment whilst competing in other disciplines such as road running, cross country or track and field. However, if you do train regularly on trail or fell then at some point the temptation to race over it and really test yourself will be too hard to bear.

3.1 Choosing and entering an event:

The first step to entering an event is finding out about it. Here there can be differences between trail runs and fell runs.

Trail runs tend to be closer to the more main-stream road races with the organisers coming from the general athletics background. You will find entry forms in sports shops and at races, with adverts for the races in running magazines and other publications. In addition, details of those races registered with them can be found on the TRA website.

Fell runs can be more of a closed shop and normally aren't advertised heavily. Each year in December/January the FRA issue a fixtures calendar of all events registered with them for the coming year. This goes out to all members of the FRA and allows them to plan their year's racing. For the runner serious about fell running then they really must join the FRA. As with the TRA, brief details of upcoming fell races can be found on the FRA website. The same applies with the relevant bodies for Northern Ireland, Scotland and Wales.

Similar to fell races, LDWA events aren't really advertised anywhere. Again members of the LDWA find out about events through the members' newsletter known as "The Strider".

On both trail and fell races the safety of the runner is of paramount importance and it is the race organiser's responsibility to design a course that does not present undue dangers to the runner. However, as with all outdoor activities the primary responsibility for safety lies with the runner themselves.

All races in the outdoor environment have risks associated with them and the rougher the terrain and more remote the location then the higher the risk factor. The competitor must ensure that they are aware of the type of event that they are entering and ensure that they have the necessary physical preparation, skills and relevant equipment to meet the challenge provided by the event.

EOD, Most events do accept – Enter On the Day, but some may charge an additional fee for this late entry. The majority of fell races are entry on day only. Be aware that those events, both trail and fell, with closing dates and/or restrictions on numbers of runners may not allow EOD. Always check the form and never assume. Championship events, both trail and fell, normally attract large fields and so are usually pre-entry only. LDWA events are usually pre-entry.

Unattached fees.

On this subject trail and fell races are totally opposite. Similar to road races, trail races normally charge an additional fee for those runners who don't belong to a recognised club. Fell races don't, there is the one fee whether you belong to a club or not.

> **Length of races**
> See section 4 Endurance Work. Due to the increased physical demands on the body do not assume that you can comfortably run the same distances as you can on the road.

The reason for the difference is down to the way that each of the governing bodies attract their funding. The TRA do not charge race organisers who belong to affiliated clubs a fee for issuing the race permit and insurance. The income for the TRA comes from the levy charged to non-club runners in addition to the race entry fee. This passed from the race organiser to the TRA.

With fell running, on the other hand, the FRA charge the race organiser a fee for issuing the race permit and insurance. This is then passed onto the competitor through the race entry fee. There is no requirement imposed by the FRA on the organiser to charge non-club runners an unattached levy.

Age categories.

As you'll know athletics has a number of age categories for both male and female runners. As the runner grows older they move up an age category. These age categories are in five year increments however many races, because of smaller fields and therefore prize lists, operate a ten year increment.

With male runners both trail and fell running operate the same as the other athletic disciplines with the senior male moving up into the veteran category on his 40th birthday.

With female runners there is a difference between the way that trail and fell categorise vets. In mainstream athletics, unlike a male, a senior female turns into the vet category on her 35th birthday. Trail running follows suit with the female athlete becoming a vet at 35 and then moving up the corresponding age increments, i.e. 35, 45, 55. With fell running there is no difference in the treatment of male and female athletes. Both sexes move into the veteran classes at 40.

It is worth bearing this in mind when completing your race entry form.

Qualifying races.

Some events, trail, fell and LDWA have a requirement for the runner to have completed a specified event or type of event before their entry will be accepted.

These are normally the more "challenging" events either through length of distance or the physical difficulties associated with completing the course or even both. The entry requirements are there to assess whether you have both the physical fitness and abilities to complete the course. In some cases documentary proof such as race results may be required as verification.

Compulsory kit.
Some events have a mandatory kit list that must be carried. This may be enforced by kit checks before, during and after the event. This kit list is whatever the event organiser judges to be the minimum equipment to be carried by the competitor to help ensure their survival in the event of any unforeseen incidents. Ensure that you are carrying it.
The kit list will vary from event to event depending on the time of the year, the remoteness and the type of terrain being covered, the distance involved and the level of support provided by the event. Generally more kit will be required for a winter event in mountainous terrain than for a summer one along a canal towpath.
See Section 5 : Required kit for events.

3.2 Grading of routes:

There is no definitive grading system in the UK that has been adopted across the full spectrum of off-road running.

Neither the Trail Runner's Association nor the LDWA have ever put any form of grading system in place.

With regard to fell running, the FRA have had a grading system for a number of years that applies solely to those events registered for fell running. This works by grading a race by its toughness and then combining this with the distance of the event. Each event is categorised as A, B or C with category A being the hardest and C being the least severe.

Category A
1. should average not less than 250 feet/76 metres of climbing for every mile ran.
2. should not have more than 20% of its distance on road.
3. should be at least one mile in length.

Category B
1. should average not less than 125 feet /38 metres of climbing for every mile ran.
2. should not have more than 30% of this distance on road.

Category C
1. should average not less than 100 feet /30.4 metres of climbing for every mile ran.
2. should not have more than 40% of the race distance on road.

3. should contain some genuine fell terrain.

The race lengths are categorised as follows
L - long race is 12 miles (19.3 km) or over.
M - medium race is 6 miles (9.6 km) and over but under 12 miles (19.3 km).
S - short race is under 6 miles (9.6 km).

Races are then graded using a mix of these two combinations of letters. For example, an AL race would be one that was over twelve miles and contained an average of over 250 feet of ascent for each mile of the race i.e. for a 12 mile race over 3000 feet of climbing. Whereas a 5 mile race with 600 feet of climbing would be categorised as a CS with it having 120 feet of climbing per mile and being under six miles.

In addition, the following abbreviations are used to give additional information about fell races.

ER which means "experience required"- basically not a race for beginners due to it's severity.
LK, meaning that "local knowledge" of the route would be an advantage to the runners.
NS, the route is not marked and "navigational skills" are required.
PM, the route is partially marked. See section 6-Route Finding, Waymarking and Navigation for further clarification on this.

There are two further categories of fell race.
Category O which is an orienteering style event held in fell or mountain terrain.
Category MM which is a mountain marathon type event.
As navigation and route finding is a crucial element of these two categories of event then the length of run, amount of height climbed and severity of terrain covered will depend on the particular route chosen by the competitors.

3.3 Using the Grading System for progression of ability:

For the new comer to off-road running, it can be difficult to judge what races are within both their physical and experience capability. Many beginners to fell running may have experience in this environment coming from a hill walking background or similar. Others wouldn't have and the whole situation may be unfamiliar and new. By using the FRA's grading scale on a positive basis it is possible to build a programme that will expand both your physical abilities and your experience and awareness of the fell/ mountain environment.

The first rule on this is to both listen and to ignore your club mates and running friends who are more experienced than you in this discipline of running. Listen to them for advice and guidance and learn from their experience. Ignore them when they recommend entering a race with which you are not comfortable and feel is beyond your current ability. The enthusiasm of running friends to draw you into their world, and without any malice on their part, can be infectious and encourage you into an event for which you are not ready.

Use the grading system to progress yourself. Start competing at the CS and BS rating level. Once you feel confident and comfortable at this level then move up to the CM and BM level. From there try an AS event then maybe a CL or BL. Never move up to an AM until you have completed at least two CL or BL events. An AL event should be a no-no until you have done at least two AM races and are a confident navigator. As above, the beginner to fell running should stick to those courses that are marked until they are confident in their ability to navigate.

The FRA organise regular courses on navigation and safety on fells. See the FRA website for details. Other bodies also organise navigation and awareness courses for adventure runners and competitors in navigation-style races. For the beginner to the sport the knowledge and self-confidence that can be gained from enrolling on these courses can be extremely beneficial.

3.4 How many events should I do in a year:

With off-road running you may be surprised at how often you can compete. While running on the trails and the fells can be physically demanding in some respects, in others it can be a lot easier.

The biggest limiting factor when road running is impact shock, the force that is generated from your feet hitting the hard surface of the road and which is then transmitted up your leg. Obviously when running on a softer surface such as trail or fell this shock factor is substantially reduced. This puts the legs under less pressure with the result that the committed off-road runner can compete on a more regular basis than the road runner with fewer injury risks.

It is not unknown for the fell and trail runner to compete every week for long periods of time. Some runners have even been known to compete several times per week for short periods. By using your head and not totally over-doing it, it is possible to get greater enjoyment out of competing in trail and fell races on a more regular basis than you possibly can road running.

4. Physical Aspects of Trail and Fell Running.

Not many people from a non-running background make the sudden decision to try trail and fell running. It is a relatively safe assumption that those who are either contemplating trying or are new to off-road running have come from one of the other running disciplines and in all probability road running. As such they will be aware of the physical demands that running places on the participant. But what of the additional physical requirements over and above what would be the norm for, say, the average road runner. This section looks at these additional demands.

4.1 Running style:

The classic endurance running style is all about running as fast as possible while using the least amount of energy. This tends to give a running style with the arms close to the side and moving backwards and forwards, slightly crossing the body. At the same time the body is held vertical with a slight lean forwards. Stride length is not too long and the thigh is not lifted as high as in fast paced running with the foot skimming just above the running surface. When running off- road this classic style still holds true as being the most energy efficient method of running. However there are sections in every off-road race where this energy efficient style has to be modified and changed. In certain circumstances the most economical running style is not the most practical or efficient. Practical examples of this are .

1. Running down hill where the arms are used for balance and where the stride length and head and body position may be altered.

2. Running uphill where there is a greater lean forward into the hill and arms will pump more vigorously to help power legs.

3. Running across uneven terrain where high vegetation may force the runner to adopt a higher than normal knee lift.

4. Running across uneven terrain where the runner may be constantly having to change stride length, unlike the road runner who gets into a constantly repeating rhythm.

The off-road runner may be constantly changing running pattern to meet changing ground conditions. In these circumstances it makes logical sense to adapt their training schedule to include exercises that will improve the ability to change running pattern both quickly and constantly.

Stable and Unstable Ground

In this guide the terms stable and unstable ground are often mentioned. In order to make the most effective use of his running stride the runner needs to place his/her foot on a hard level surface. This will enable them to make the most use of their energy and power to push themselves away from the ground on the take-off stage off the stride. The classic examples of a hard level running surface are athletics tracks and roads. These are considered to be stable surfaces.

In the off-road world nothing is as stable as these two although such surfaces as forest roads and well-made vehicle tracks can be considered as stable. Any other ground can be considered as being unstable to various degrees because it does not allow the runner to make the maximum use of his/her energy and power. This may be due to the ground being soft and absorbing energy or being uneven and/or loose and not allowing the runner to push-off in a straight line or it could be any combination of the two. Because of this, running on unstable ground is naturally slower than on stable ground.

All off-road running is classed as running on unstable ground. For the off-road runner, the choice is finding the least unstable ground to run over in order to make the most effective use of his/her running action.

4.2 Strength:

Running off-road places certain stresses on the body over and above those encountered during normal running. Starting at the bottom we'll look at the various muscle groups in turn and establish what these stresses are.

Ankles

Starting right at the bottom of the leg, the ankle. The optimum running position has the foot and ankle pushing away from the ground after landing. This push is best done in a straight line with the foot and ankle level and providing a stable support for the push. In road and track running the running surface is relatively level and stable and therefore no great problem for pushing off. However with off-road running the foot will probably land on an uneven surface and as it lands will roll in one direction or another. In order to control this roll and prevent the body over-balancing resulting in a fall, the ankle muscles will compensate to bring the ankle back into a level position during push-off to maintain the straight ahead direction of travel. This compensation obviously works the ankle muscles and ligaments a lot more than just normal running. Stiff and sore ankles are quite often the result of running over rough, uneven ground.

The ankles can also suffer during downhill running. The effect of gravity as you run downhill is increased compared to flat running because of the angle of descent, the leg falls a little bit further than normal on each stride. This means that the ankle suffers a little bit more stress and impact shock than during normal running.

Buttock muscles
The buttock is comprised of three muscles,
1. Large
2. Intermediate
3. Small

These muscles are used a lot more during off-road running compared to road running. The large buttock muscle powers the backward drive of the leg and this is heavily used when running uphill. The intermediate and the small buttock muscles stabilise the hip and restrain the upper body preventing it folding inwards on every stride. These are heavily used while running down hill as gravity and the angle of the descent combine to give increased stride length.

Groin muscles
The groin muscle or to be more precise the adductors work quite powerfully as the foot leaves the ground and starts to swing forward. During this swing, the leg rotates outwards in relation to the hip. The adductors then come into play and swing the leg back towards the midline of the body. Additional pressure is placed on the adductors when side stepping or suddenly changing direction. Occurrences that do not happen during road running but which are common movements when running off-road.

Thigh muscles
The thigh muscles or quadriceps (quads) are used during running to prevent excessive knee flexion. When running, gravity pulls the knee downwards on every foot strike, this is known as knee flexion. Due to the angle of descent, the quads can be put under considerable pressure when running downhill. As the proportion of downhill running is that much higher during trail and fell compared to road running the stresses that the quads are placed under is also considerably higher.

Calf muscles
The calf muscles are very important for running. They bend both the knee and the ankles so that the body can be raised on to it's toes during the push-off stage of the running action. Additional strain can be placed in these through coping with running on uneven terrain and up and down slopes.

Trunk and upper body muscles
In the normal running action the trunk remains almost erect with only a slight forward lean, while the arms assist the running action by balancing the rhythm of the

legs.

When running off-road this all changes. The trunk muscles, both back and abdominal, are used more often as there is a much higher movement of the body compared to road running. This is due to the balancing action from having to run across uneven ground and particularly due to the fact that the additional stresses placed on the other muscle groups ultimately all run through the core of the body, the trunk.

Again the arms and shoulders have a much higher rate of movement than compared to road running. This ranges from being pumped backwards and forwards to help power uphill movement to being carried in the outstretched position to aid balance while descending.

4.3 Energy consumption:

One of the most heard comments from beginners to off-road running is how tired they feel after a race. More tired than after a corresponding road run. A large chunk of this is down to the increased energy demands that is placed on the body by off-road running compared to running on the road or track, but what causes this extra need for energy. The answer to this is down to three factors.

1. As part of the motion of running the body lands on one foot and then immediately pushes away again to take-off for the next stride. This push and take-off requires an explosive force which in turn requires energy to power it. Part of the energy comes from the bounce-back effect of the foot hitting the ground. The harder the surface, the stronger this bounce-back effect. Correspondingly the softer the surface the weaker the bounce-back. This happens at the moment the foot impacts the ground. A softer surface will absorb more of the impact force than a harder one resulting in a weaker bounce-back. The weaker bounce-back means that the runner has to expend more of their energy to lift their legs. This may not seem much but consider how many times the runner lifts the legs during the course of a run and it soon mounts up. As a practical example of this principle take a rubber ball and bounce it on a concrete floor and then bounce it on a grass field. On which surface does the ball bounce higher and farther ??

2. By its very nature running off-road crosses more unstable ground than roads or track running. In order to keep the body in an upright position there needs to be some compensating use of other muscle groups. It is often not fully understood by runners that there is an increased demand of the core muscle groups such as the abdominal and upper and lower back. In addition to this there is an increased usage of the arm and shoulder muscles for both balance and to power up hill

running. In short this means that you are using more muscle groups during the activity of off-road running and this usage requires energy.

3. Be it trail or fell there is nearly always more hills than there are in a corresponding road run. Uphill running requires more energy than level running. In reality the concept of what you lose on the uphills, you'll get back on the downhills does not apply. When compared to running on the level, running up an incline of 6% [6 metres of vertical climb per hundred metres of level distance] will use 35% more energy. On the other side running downhill on the same slope only reduces the effort by 25%, a mismatch of 9% of the runners energy consumption. As you can see the hillier the course the higher the cost in energy expenditure.

Ok, so off-road uses more energy but what effect does that have on training and competition.

Keeping things fairly simple, the primary fuel for all exercise is carbohydrates. This is converted into Adenosine Triphosphate or ATP which is the actual fuel for the explosive muscle contraction which powers all movement. Once the body's store of carbohydrate is exhausted the body then changes fuel source to run on fat reserves, however fat is a much less efficient fuel source than carbohydrate and can result in a significant difference in performance levels.

For normal running the average runner holds enough carbohydrates in their body for 90 minutes of exercise. As we've seen above off-road running has a higher energy consumption than normal running. Therefore the carbohydrate reserve will be consumed before the 90 minutes is reached. The body will start switching to using fat reserves a lot sooner than on a corresponding road run. The rougher and more physically demanding the course, the higher the energy usage and the sooner carbohydrate reserves are depleted. Off-road running is therefore much more endurance based than even regular long distance running and needs to be trained for as such. This training may mean a higher proportion of endurance (long runs) sessions and may also include practising replenishing energy stores while on the run.

4.4 Slow running and walking:

One of the fundamental criteria of all endurance running is getting the best performance out of the bodies limited energy stores. The most effective way of doing this is even paced running. Top quality runners are capable of churning out times where the mile splits are within seconds of each other.

Unfortunately even paced running is totally dependant upon having an even running course and surface in front of you. If there is a large hill to go up or come down or a rough running surface to cross then it becomes very difficult to maintain an even pace. By their very nature off-road courses will always contain elements that will force the runner to constantly change pace. Each course will have sections where the runner will be able to run fast and where they will be forced slow the pace and maybe even walk. It then becomes important to factor the ability to pace change into the runners training.

To anybody participating in road running there is a self-imposed mental disgrace about walking. This is probably due to the fact that a road race is more accessible to spectators and self-pride prevents any walking in front of them.

With off-road running there is a different attitude. In both trail and, especially, fell races there maybe sections of the route where it is just too inefficient to attempt to run and it makes more sense to walk. This may be down to the nature of the ground being crossed such as overgrown vegetation i.e. deep heather or more likely down to the fact that the hill is just too long and steep to run up.

4.5 Load carrying:

Although not usual in competition, there may still be a requirement for the road runner to carry drinks or waterproofs during training. With the off-road runner there is a definite requirement to carry drinks and equipment during both training and competition. This additional load will vary depending on the event and the equipment required. However carrying additional weight of any size will impose higher physical demands upon the runner. Load carrying will effect the running style, endurance capacity, energy consumption, running speed and strength requirements.

4.6 Suppleness:

As with all runners a regular general stretching routine or even possibly a yoga session will provide enough flexibility for the off-road runner. However there are three areas that do warrant extra attention and need to be included in any stretching routine.

Upper body stretches.
As we have seen the trunk, back and shoulders play a more prominent part in off-road running. It is surprising how many runners neglect to include stretching exercises for these areas into their routine. This needs to be done. Try the simple exercises below.

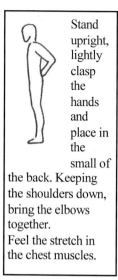 Stand upright, lightly clasp the hands and place in the small of the back. Keeping the shoulders down, bring the elbows together. Feel the stretch in the chest muscles.

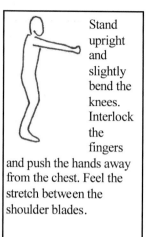 Stand upright and slightly bend the knees. Interlock the fingers and push the hands away from the chest. Feel the stretch between the shoulder blades.

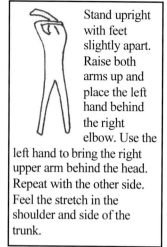 Stand upright with feet slightly apart. Raise both arms up and place the left hand behind the right elbow. Use the left hand to bring the right upper arm behind the head. Repeat with the other side. Feel the stretch in the shoulder and side of the trunk.

Quads.

Most runners do include quad stretching exercises into their routine. However, as explained previously, off-road running makes a considerably heavier demand on the quads than other forms of running. This gives a greater importance to these exercises.

Groin

The groin area or to be specific the adductor muscles play a major part in all running activities. However both trail and fell running place a particular stress on them due to side-stepping or sudden changes in direction when competing off-road. This can over-exert these muscles and give considerable discomfort in the groin area, often called a groin strain. This over-exertion is mainly caused by an inflexibility of these muscles. Incorporating specific exercises into your stretching routine will help act as a preventative against any possible injuries. There are two simple exercises that are easy to perform and will greatly increase mobility in this area.

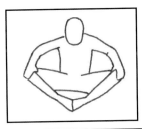

| Sit with the soles of the feet together. Use the hands to slowly press the knees down. You'll start to feel the stretch in the adductors. Hold for 30 seconds. Never push down with the hands to the point where it becomes painful. | Sit with your legs wide apart. Place your hands on the upper thigh. Slowly bend forward from the waist running your hands down the top of your legs. Feel the stretch and hold for 30 seconds. Again never perform to the point of pain. |

This is an introduction to the specific requirements of mobility exercises for off-road runners. A more detailed analysis of why, how and how often we should stretch is contained in the sister booklet " Strength and Conditioning for Off– Road Runners".

5. Training for Trail and Fell Running.

5.1 General training principles:

Ask any coach and they will tell you that the first rule of any training is that of being specific. That means making the training specific to the type of competition that you are entering. In the case of off-road running then you have to gear your training to off-road as well.

With the exception of terrain training all of the methods below are standard sessions that the majority of runners use for improvement just slanted towards off-road running as opposed to road or track. Terrain training is specific to off-road running and is geared to conditioning the body to the different stresses encountered when running over different terrain.

As this book is classed as an introduction to the sport, it only covers the basic details of these training methods for the beginner to off-road running. For further details and more detailed training sessions see the relevant sister publications from this series.

Uphill Techniques for Off-Road Runners
Downhill Techniques for Off-Road Runners
Speed Training for Off-Road Runners
Terrain Training for Off-Road Runners
Strength and Conditioning for Off-Road Runners

5.2 Endurance work:

As we have stated previously off-road running is more energy expensive than other forms of running. As the whole crux of endurance work, be it for trail, fell, road or track is to make the runner more energy efficient then it is a vital part of training for off-road events.

The bog standard endurance session for most runners is the weekly long distance run and for the off-road runner this is no different. However what is different, is that as much as possible, this long session needs to be done over the same type of terrain as you expect to race over. A weekly long 16 mile road run, while improving your endurance, will not adequately prepare you for a trail run over the South Downs or a fell race in the Lakes.

As we have described before there are subtle differences required from the body for off-road running compared to running on tarmac, such as the neuromuscular adaptations to running on rough terrain. While these can be prepared and improved during shorter off-road runs the ability to perform these for long distances or time periods can only be done by running off-road for long distances.

So how far should these endurance runs be. As a general rule of thumb you should be capable of running over similar terrain to your race distance plus 50%. So if you are training to race a distance of six miles then you should be capable of comfortably running a nine mile distance over a similar terrain as the race. During the long training run, other sessions can be included to improve the training benefits of the run such as including rolling hills or inserting a fifteen to twenty minute threshold session.

5.3 Uphill work:

Nearly all runners do some form of hill work even track runners. It is a fundamental exercise for developing strength and endurance for the runner. However for the off-road runner this has a particular emphasise due to the simple fact that during trail and fell runs you are much more likely to spend a major portion of the race running up hills than in other running disciplines.

The prime requisite for all hill running is leg strength. This can be built up just by including hilly runs within your weekly long run However the most effective and quickest way of improving your hill climbing ability is to include a specific hill rep session within your training schedule.

Obviously hill running is quite demanding due to the amount of climb and rougher terrain. As far as possible it is always advisable to train over similar types of hill and terrain as you expect to race over.

As well as the physical conditioning that is required for hill running there are other skill factors that need to be considered such as :

1. Angle of lean
2. Balance
3. Breathing
4. Eye/foot co-ordination
5. Foot plant
6. Pace judgment
7. Stamina
8. Stride length
9. Taking a line and route choice
10. Transition between different angles of slope
11. Walking

5.4 Downhill work:

The vast majority of trail and fell races have an element of downhill running, this makes downhill running a crucial part of the runner's training regime. However it is surprising how few runners will put the effort in to train specifically for downhill running. Virtually everyone will do hill rep sessions concentrating on the uphills but do the same to practice the downhills .... nah!

The logic of this is surprising. A great many runners think that this is unnecessary as running downhill is easy, you just point and go. This is a totally wrong attitude. There are many factors that need to be taken into account while descending especially the rougher the terrain and more unstable the running surface. However the biggest problem with downhill running is the physical demands that it places on the body. After running a particularly hilly course many runners complain of a soreness in the legs particularly the quads, that they attribute to unaccustomed uphill running. In reality this is actually caused by the effort of coming down rather than going up.

When running downhill the quadriceps (quads) muscles work eccentrically which puts the muscles under considerable stress which can result in damage to the quads. These stresses can be adapted to by regular downhill training. However not only does the runner have to condition the body for the physical demands of running downhill but there is also the skill element as well that needs to be practiced. This consists of the following elements.
1. Route choice.
2. Balance.
3. Eye/foot co-ordination.
4. Angle of lean.
5. Stride length.
6. Foot plant.
7. Stamina/lactic build-up.
8. Transition between degrees of slope.

As can be seen, effective downhill running is more technical than just "point and go".

5.5 Speed work:

At the end of the day, with competitive running the basic idea is to get round the course in as fast a time as possible whether the race be road, track, fell or trail. In order to do this the runner needs to practise fast paced running. As with other running disciplines that are endurance based there are two elements to increasing your running speed.

1. Increase your natural basic running speed.
2. Increasing the ability of maintaining that speed for long periods over long distances.

However with off-road running there is an additional third element and that is maintaining a high speed for long periods over long distances on rough terrain.

In order to improve speed, the majority of runners do some form of speed work such as reps or intervals. Off-road runners should be no exception. Speed work should be an essential part of their training just as much as a track runner. However in order for the body to adapt to running fast over rough terrain then speed sessions need to be performed over the similar kind of terrain.

However this needs to be tempered by the basic philosophy of why we train for speed work. In order to run fast we need to train fast, the faster you can train then the more productive the speed work will be. As we have already shown, for various reasons, running off-road is slower than running on an athletics track or running on the road. Concentrating purely on running over trail and fell will not help the off-road runner achieve their potential in terms of gaining speed.

In order to run fast the runner needs to practice running fast and the fastest surface to run on is an athletics track. This then gives a quandary. In order to develop the body's ability to run fast over rough terrain then the runner must do speed work on rough terrain but at the same time in order to maintain or improve their basic speed the runner also needs to perform speed sessions on the athletic track. If an athletics track is not available then road based sessions can be used.

For the time-stretched average runner having to cope with other training demands then one session per week of speed work will be adequate. This can be split week and week about with the session being held on a running track one week and on terrain the following week etc, etc.

Keeping all the scientific mumbo-jumbo such as anaerobic, aerobic etc, to a minimum, speed work can be basically split into three types.

1. Pure speed,
2. Speed endurance.
3. Threshold (lactic tolerance)

Pure speed.
The idea here is that you will have a given speed for, say, a five mile run. If you break this five miles down into shorter distances and put a recovery break at the end of these shorter runs, then you can run this five mile in an overall faster time than if you ran the five mile continuously. By increasing your running pace over these

shorter distances then this will also reduce your average running time over longer distances. For the endurance runner the classic speed session is the 5 k or 3 mile session. Here the 5k is broken down into 12 x 400 metre runs with a recovery ratio of 1:1. This means that the recovery time between intervals is equal to the time it took to complete the run. As fitness improves then the running time will be cut and correspondingly so will the recovery time.

Variations of this basic 12 x 400 metres can be performed such as 6 x 800 metres and 24 x 200 metres. However each rep should be done at between 85 to 90% of the runners best time for the distance of the rep.

Speed endurance.

Speed endurance is the ability to run at a fast pace for long periods. This is normally achieved by using longer training distances with relatively shorter recovery periods. Typically the distances ran are from 800 metres to 3,000 metres with the recovery time of 50% of the time taken to run the rep.

A standard session of this type is 6 x 1 mile reps run at a pace slightly faster than your 10k race pace. The recovery would be half the time taken to run the rep. As with the speed sessions variations on this standard can be used such as 4 x 3,000 metres, 5 x 2,000 metres etc.

Threshold

These sessions are used to develop the body's ability to handle the build-up of lactic acid within the muscles. This type of session is normally performed by a fast-paced distance run. Around twenty minutes of continuous running at just under 10k race pace or 80 - 85% of maximum heart rate.

For the off-road runner this session is still very appropriate but can be transferred to a more relevant undulating trail or fell setting. The terrain should be undulating rather than hilly as this will help ensure the continuity of pace without the leg muscles tying- up.

5.6 Terrain training:

Terrain training is training the body and its neurological responses to landing the foot onto rough unstable ground. This ground may have the consistency of hard packed earth all the way through to the soggy, clinging mess of a peat bog. Once landed the foot must then be used for pushing the runner forward before being lifted up ready to be placed for the next step.

The ideal running situation is where the foot lands on a hard level surface. As it is a level surface there are no distractions and the body's muscles will react through the

Above. Mud. Something that can be expected on almost every trail and fell race. The only thing that varies is the depth.

There are not many trail or fell races in which hills do not play some significance. As a result they have to become a fundamental feature of your training and hill reps need to be included on a regular basis within your training schedule.

foot to push off in a straight line upwards and forwards. Complications arise on rough and uneven surfaces where the foot makes contact with the ground at odd angles other than flat on the floor. This causes the body to "roll" with the distinct danger of over-balancing and falling. To counter this the small muscles around the ankle joint compensate and act as buffers to prevent the body from rolling too far. This obviously puts these muscles under stress and for the runner unaccustomed to running off –road can give considerable ankle soreness.

The ability to run fast over rough ground is obviously linked to leg strength, mobility and eye/ foot co-ordination. However other factors that come into play when running across rough and unstable surfaces include.
1. High knee lifts to counter tall vegetation such as heather, rushes etc.
2. The ability to change stride length quickly to cope with changing surfaces.
3. The ability to side-step and change direction suddenly.
4. How to place the foot when landing on different surfaces such as mud, ice, rocks etc.
5. How to recognise different running surfaces and the hazards that they present.
6. Passing hazards safely for example crossing streams , loose scree etc.
7. Balance.
8. The ability to plant the foot without putting the full body weight on it.
9. Walking.

These factors can all be adapted to by practicing and training over suitable ground. Including elements of this type of training into your schedule will not go amiss. These elements can be combined with other training factors such as up and/or downhill work to give, for example, a downhill session over rough terrain.

5.7 Strength work:

All runners need strength. At the end of the day, running is a weight bearing activity just as much as weight lifting. The fact that the runner is moving and that the weight involved is the runner's own body weight tends to mask the fact that the runner is still lifting weight up and down. And in the runners case, over a considerable amount of repartitions and over a considerable amount of time.

Most runners perform no strength work other than running itself. This is a mistake especially for those contemplating trying their hand at off-road running. As previously shown there is a greater all-round need for strength for the off-road runner but what other reasons demand a degree of strength training.

1. All muscles work in pairs, where one provides the power, the other supports it. For example, as the quads shorten, the hamstrings lengthen. Depending purely upon running for strength work will only really strengthen those muscle groups directly

related to the running action. It will not necessarily strengthen the supporting muscle groups to the same extent. This leads to an imbalance between muscles with the supporting muscle not really having the ability to support the major muscle group in action. The result = injury. A general all round strength programme will help prevent these imbalances.

2. Stronger muscles tire less easily than weak ones. Off-road running is an endurance based activity. Stronger muscles tire slower and increase the endurance capacity of the athlete.

So what strengthening exercises are best for the trail and fell runner. There are numerous strength exercises out there, some routines are to build specific muscle groups, others provide a general all-round fitness. As a relative beginner to off-road running it may be more advisable for the reader to follow a general circuit training programme rather than practise more specific exercises.

The following circuit is one that can be quite easily be done at home. The individual exercises are very appropriate for the movement patterns that you will encounter during trail and fell running. Perform once a week for 20 to 30 minutes. If performed correctly it can be an excellent form of aerobic training and can quite easily replace one of your weekly steady runs in your training schedule with no adverse effect on your endurance ability. In fact it could increase it.

1. 15 x Quick Squats   2. 12 x Press-ups   3. 10 x Sit-ups

4. 8 x Burpees   5. 8 x Back Arches

| 6. 20 x High Knee Running Steps | 7. 12 x Vertical Jumps |

The exercises are quite energetic so don't perform on your best carpet. Sweat stains !

Progression
Perform each exercise the stated number of times moving straight from one to the next with no recovery between each exercise. When all the exercises have been performed, that is one set. At the end of one set take a recovery equal in time to 50% of the time it took you to complete the set. Then start the next set. Initially perform two sets, then after four weeks move up to three sets, then after another four weeks move up to four sets. Perform these exercises during the general training phase of your programme. Do not perform in the week leading up to the race.

5.8 Constructing a session:

Most runners especially club runners, know the benefits of including quality sessions within their training schedule. This is no different for the off-road runner. Sessions similar in style to those used by the road and track runner can be constructed, the only difference being that they are slanted more towards the demands of the trail and fell runner.

The prime example of this is the hill rep. Most runners include hill reps of some kind into their training with, normally, a hill session every month or couple of weeks. With running off-road, hills have a much greater prominence and therefore a weekly hill session would then become more appropriate. Also the quantity and length of the rep would be increased in line with the demands of the off-road runner.

Typical sessions that would be utilised would include

1. Hill Reps, both up and down.
2. Up and Downhill Reps.
3. Fartlek.
4. Pyramids.

5. Rolling Hills.
6. Undulating Speed Runs.
7. Undulating Threshold Runs.

1. Hill reps. The bog standard sessions as used by most runners consisting of running up a hill hard and then taking a recovery on the way back down. This can also be used in reverse with the effort being put in on the downhill leg thus giving a downhill rep session.

2. Up and down hill reps. A variation on normal hill reps but instead of taking the recovery on the way back down, the effort is continued on the downhill after the climb. The recovery is taken as a rest before starting up the next hill.

> All intervals or repartitions within a session whether it is speed, speed endurance, uphill or downhill, should be done with the same intensity of effort. i.e. the time for the last rep should be more or less the same as for the first. Effectively even paced running throughout the session.

3. Fartlek. Fartlek is an ideal training method for off road running be it trail or fell. The fast/ slow style of running mirrors the running pattern of what actually happens in most off-road races. Unlike road races where the optimum tactic is to keep an even pace throughout the race, the nature of off-road courses means that the pace is constantly varying either because of hills, the nature of the ground or even weather conditions.

4. Pyramids. A pyramid session is a series of reps of varying distance typically along the lines of 200 metres, 300 metres, 400 metres. The idea is to run the 200 metres with effort, recover back to the start, run the 300 metres with effort, recover back to the start, run the 400 metres with effort, recover back to the start, run the 300 metres with effort, recover back to the start, run the 200 metres with effort, recover back to the start and then go back up the scale again.

They are a standard session for track and road runners but can easily be adapted by the off-road runner by performing them in more rugged terrain especially as uphill and downhill sessions.

5. Rolling hills. These can be incorporated into a long and/or steady run. Plan the route carefully to take in hills of a similar nature that you want to train for and treat the climbs and/or the descents as you would on a hill session. The recovery would

> When doing this form of speed work over rough terrain it is advisable not to include any steep uphill or downhill sections on the route. Undulating ground is sufficient and is advisable to train on. Steep hills can be left for the uphill and downhill sessions.

result from slowing the pace down after the effort.

6. Undulating speed runs. Similar in nature to the runner's rep or interval session except that they would be performed over undulating ground as opposed to an athletics track. It is important to ensure that the uphills do not get too long or steep. Momentum must be ensured without the leg muscles tying up. Distances can range from 200 metres to 3000 metres.

7. Undulating threshold runs. Similar to the undulating speed run except that the effort is between twenty to thirty minutes of continuous running. This session is used to develop lactic tolerance. The pace for the effort would be just short of 10 K race pace and would equate to 90% of maximum heart rate.

5.9 Length of sessions :

As a generalisation each of the sessions from 1 to 4 plus 6 can be performed over the following time periods. Which one you would choose would depend upon your particular need at a particular time. If your need is to develop speed then the shorter sessions should be given a greater priority. If the need is for greater strength and endurance then your training should tip towards the longer sessions.

Short reps of between 30 and 60 seconds running time can be used to develop the use of technique and style. The short length means that a particular attribute such as holding the arms out for balance can be practiced, without the session being that long that concentration begins to waver. Many repetitions of short duration will help ingrain the correct running style into the body's movement pattern.
One other use of short hill reps is to help develop eccentric muscle strength. For short distances it is possible to really attack the gradient whether it is up or down. It would be recommended to only do this session on a shallow slope with a good soft running surface such as grass.
For a skills session, the emphasis should be on practicing technique rather than running fast. A typical session would normally be between 20 to 30 reps broken down into 2 or 3 sets with a short recovery in between. This helps prevent concentration fatigue. For the more power based session, this would normally entail 3 sets of 8 reps with an easy jog/walk back as the recovery between reps and a 5 to 7 minute easy recovery run between sets.

Medium reps of between 2 to 5 minutes will help aerobic capacity. A number of different sessions of this length representing different running surfaces and angles of climb and/or descent should be built up. Normally sessions of this type will comprise of between 10 to 15 reps with an easy jog/walk back as the recovery.

Long reps of over 5 minutes can be used to develop the body's ability to maintain pace and concentration. Runners often use this type of session on a level surface but for the off-road runner this also needs to be done on the hills. Hills with a climbing or descent time of longer than 5 minutes will be encountered in races. Therefore it should be no surprise that you should prepare for them.

Being practical the number of reps will depend upon the length of the hill. You can't say, do 10 reps if the total time of going up and coming back down for each rep is going to be 30 minutes. The more logical way of looking at this is to keep the session to 60 minutes excluding warm-up and warm-down. Do as many reps as will fit into the 60 minutes.

An effective use of these sessions would be to split the year into training and competitive phases. During the training phase a greater emphasise would be placed on developing strength and endurance. Then as the year moves towards the competitive phase the emphasise will move towards speed development with the shorter sessions gradually replacing the longer ones.

This process is known as periodisation. Although practised by the more elite athletes the average runner enjoys the participation in races too much to spend long periods of the year without racing. However there may be periods of three or four weeks between races where a different training emphasis can be applied, to better prepare you for the forthcoming race.

	Quality session 1	Quality session 2	
Week 4	Long Hill Rep	Long Speed Rep	
Week 3	Long Hill Rep	Medium Speed Rep	
Week 2	Medium Hill Rep	Short Speed Rep	
Week 1	Short Hill Rep	Reduced Short Speed Rep 50% of normal volume	Race

5.10 Putting it all together:

With all these different types of session it can be difficult for a normal runner with a home, family and work to fit it all in. There is always going to be some element of comprise between what you would like to do and what you can actually do.

Expanding on the four week macrocycle shown above, a typical schedule for during the training phase could look as follows.

	Week 1	Week 2	Week 3	Week 4
Monday	Slow recovery run	Slow recovery run	Slow recovery run	Slow recovery run
Tuesday	Long down-hill reps	Long uphill reps	Structured fartlek or medium up and down hill reps	Medium terrain training
Wednesday	Steady run	Steady run	Steady run	Steady run
Thursday	Long speed reps	Medium speed reps	Long speed reps	Medium speed reps
Friday	Circuit training	Circuit training	Circuit training	Circuit training
Saturday	Undulating threshold run	Undulating threshold run	Undulating threshold run	Undulating threshold run
Sunday	Long run including rolling hills	Long run including rolling hills	Long run including rolling hills	Long run including rolling hills

As you'll notice the emphasise is placed on developing endurance, stamina and strength. As time moves closer to the competition period the emphasise will slowly change and will replace some of the endurance sessions with more medium speed and faster paced work. As you move closer to the actual race date then the schedule should look more like the one below.

Note. Training schedules shown here are for general guidelines only. Although they can be used, they will not be as effective as one based upon your own personal running circumstances.

	Week 1	Week 2	Week 3	Week 4
Monday	Slow recovery run	Slow recovery run	Slow recovery run	Slow recovery run
Tuesday	Medium uphill reps	Medium downhill reps	Short hill reps - up and down	Short uphill reps
Wednesday	Steady run	Steady run	Steady run	Steady run
Thursday	Medium speed reps	Short speed reps	Medium speed reps	Reduced short speed reps 50% of normal volume
Friday	Circuit training	Circuit training 50% of normal volume	Slow recovery run	Slow recovery run
Saturday	Undulating threshold run	Undulating threshold run	Undulating threshold run at 50% distance	Rest
Sunday	Long run including rolling hills = race distance + 50%	Long run including rolling hills = race distance	Long run including rolling hills = 60 to 75% of race distance	Race

5.11 Warming-up:

To perform most effectively right at the start of the race the body needs to have reached its optimum performance temperature before the start of the race. This is slightly above the normal core temperature of approximately 37 degrees c. and this needs to be reached within ten minutes of the race starting. This is normally done by performing a warm up routine of combined mild physical and flexibility exercises leading into slightly faster but still easy running. This will raise the body's metabolism, and temperature while speeding up the circulation.

In principle every runner does this before a race. In reality the better quality runners do the full warm up, other runners will do a warm up jog at best. With off road running performing on adequate warm-up can be more important than you think, many trail runs and most fell runs have a significant hill climb close to the start. The extra increased effort required for the climb puts the body under considerable pressure before it is really ready to cope with it. This will give a considerable shock to the body's system and will mean lost time at the beginning of the run as the body struggles to adjust to the rigours of the race. An adequate warm-up will soften this shock to the system.

5.12 Mental attitude:

Having a positive mental attitude is beneficial in all running disciplines and running over trail and fell is no exception.

Running off-road presents a challenge that is over and above that faced in a normal road race and that is the challenge of completing the course. This is more-so the harder and more physically demanding that the route is. It cannot be stressed how important it is to have the belief and self-confidence to know that you can complete the race route.

The only way to build-up this belief and confidence is to practice and train for the relevant event. Standing on the start line knowing that you will complete the course is a major boost to your running capability.

You need to have:

1. Trained over the relevant distance so that you know that you can travel the full distance of the race route without undue stress and discomfort.

2. Trained over similar terrain to the event so that you know that there will be no surprises in store.

3. Trained for the uphill climbing so that you will confidently get to the top of all the hills encountered.

4. Trained for the downhill running so that you can keep your nerve and arrive safely at the bottom of all the hills.

Do all these things and not only will you achieve your target of completing the course but you will know that you can before you even start the race.

6. Technical Aspects of Trail and Fell Running.

6.1 Equipment:

So what equipment do you need to go trail and fell running. Well the answer to that is partially determined by the area in which you plan to go running. If the intention is to do a solo run through isolated mountainous terrain then you will need to be more aware of self-safety and need more kit than you would if you were running on a well-used, popular path through one of your local beauty spots.

6.1.1 Footwear:

Shoes for off-road running, both trail and fell, probably the most contentious issue among runners. Put three runners in a room to talk about this and you'll get four opinions.

First we'll look at the basic differences between shoes for running off-road and road running shoes.

The first thing that strikes you about off-road shoes is their appearance. As the shoe companies say they have a more "aggressive" outsole which provides increased grip and traction while the uppers tend to have a protective rand or bumper around the toes and reinforced stitching for durability. The foot tends to sit lower to the ground than usual compared to a road shoe in order to provide stability and responsiveness. The heel also tends to be narrower than on a corresponding road shoe for the same reason. The other main difference in appearance is the midsole. Off-road shoes usually have less cushioning than a road shoe because they are designed for a softer surface. This manifests itself in a thinner midsole and one of the reasons for the foot sitting lower to the ground. Off-road shoes tend to look "meatier" as if they mean business.

> Each type of shoe, both trail and fell, has its own merits and runners who compete on both surfaces would tend to have a pair of each so that they could use either dependant upon the course that they were running over.

Once you have got down to off-road shoes you then have the choice of type. Basically these shoes breakdown into two types, the trail running shoe and the fell running shoe. The nature of these two types can be quite different and depends upon the nature of the running surface that each were designed for. Below is a table that looks at the differences between the two followed by an analysis of the different types of running terrain that each is suitable for.

However, as always, there are provisos when choosing shoes. A race route may have

46

several different types of running surface. Ideally this may mean having several different shoes each being the best for a particular surface. Being practical it is not feasible to carry several pairs of shoes during a race and then stopping and changing during the run. So this quite often means that the shoes chosen will be a compromise as to what is the best for the overall route.

After the analysis of running terrain, there is a list of the main shoe manufacturers and which style of event they cater for. No attempt has been made to specify specific models of shoe. Manufacturers bring out new model ranges every year and such a list could quickly become outdated and inaccurate. However shoes from these manufacturers are all freely available as is information on current product ranges.

The other problem with recommending specific models is that of personal taste and fit and comfort. Everybody is different and that applies to shoe preference as well. What may fit and suit the running style of one runner may not do so for another. At the end of the day, there is no point having the most technically perfect shoe if the fit and lack of comfort cuts and hurts your feet to the point that you cannot complete the race. Better to have a technically inferior shoe that allows you to finish the run. What this means is that everybody's feet are different and what suits you may not suit someone else and vice versa. There is always going to be an element of personal trial and error when it comes down to buying running shoes whether they are fell, trail or road. The recommendation here for the newcomer to trail and fell is to go to a shop that specialises in off-road shoes and knows what they are talking about rather than the fashionable sporty shop.

6.1.2 Clothing:

Club vests
Most runners are not aware of this but under the athletic rules and regulations, if you belong to a registered athletics club then you must wear your club vest during events. There is one discipline in athletics where this is not applicable for safety reasons and that is fell running.
However, if weather conditions dictate wear a tee shirt or thermal vest under your club vest. If necessary even put a jacket over the top.

Tee shirts
Nowadays there are a lot of tee shirts on the market made from various technical fabrics that wick sweat away from the body and keep you dry. For the fell and trail runner these are far superior to the more traditional cotton tee. Cotton tends to absorb sweat as it is generated rather than wick it away with the result that you end

Trail shoe	Fell shoe
Sole Normally some variation of a square/ rectangular lug pattern. The pattern is more deeply cut than on a corresponding road shoe to provide better grip on loose and shallow mud surfaces. The sole does not dig-in to the surface in the way that a fell shoe does and so they do not provide the same level of grip on steep or soft ground. The more technically advanced trail/ adventure running shoes have a sole made from a "sticky" rubber compound to help aid grip on rocky surfaces. This "sticky" rubber can be softer than the normal rubber compound and dependant upon use, may wear quicker. The sole is designed to prevent clogging. However with a lug sole pattern it is hard to be as self-cleaning as a studded sole.	**Sole** Normally studded to provide grip on steep and/or soft ground where they can dig-in to prevent slipping. The studs may be round, square or diamond shaped depending upon manufacturer. The more technically advanced shoes have a sole made from a "sticky" rubber compound to help aid grip on rocky surfaces. This "sticky" rubber can be softer than the normal rubber compound and dependant upon use, may wear quicker. The stud pattern is normally designed to prevent clogging by mud. Effectively making them self-cleaning.
Toe-box Normally reinforced, sometimes with a rubber rand or bumper to protect against impact on stones and other objects.	**Toe-box** Normally reinforced, sometimes with a rubber rand or bumper to protect against impact on stones and other objects.
Midsole Normally of a medium height, more substantial than a fell shoe but not as high as a road shoe. This makes them not as responsive or as stable on rough ground as fell shoes. However over long distances on hard ground this extra cushioning can be very beneficial especially on stony trails. The impact absorption helps prevent soreness to the soles of the feet.	**Midsole** Minimal. The shoe is designed to keep the foot as close to the ground as possible in order to be responsive and increase stability. This also means that there is very little cushioning to protect the feet. On soft ground this presents no problem as the softness of the ground provides the cushioning. On hard ground this can cause soreness to the sole of the feet especially over long distances.

Trail shoe	Fell shoe
Upper Normally lightweight and manufactured with a mesh construction. Also normally breathable to a certain degree dependant upon manufacturer and model. Stitching tends to be reinforced for durability. The more technically advanced shoes incorporate a band around the shoe to provide additional support at minimal weight gain. The name of this band varies dependant upon manufacturer. Some models incorporate a waterproof membrane that allows sweat to wick away but prevents water entering. This tends to make the shoe heavier than normal models. It is still possible for water to enter the shoe over the ankle cuff and once in, the membrane will quite likely then prevent the water from exiting.	**Upper** Normally lightweight and manufactured with a mesh construction. Also normally breathable to a certain degree dependant upon manufacturer and model. Stitching tends to be reinforced for durability. The more technically advanced shoes incorporate a band around the shoe to provide additional support at minimal weight gain. The name of this band varies dependant upon manufacturer. Most models designed so that when the feet are wet, the movement of the foot pushes the water out through the mesh so shedding the water.
Weight Normally lighter than road shoes, although shoes incorporating a waterproof membrane may be heavier. The bulk of a shoe's weight is in its midsole and with a reduced midsole the shoe becomes lighter. As with road shoes, you do get training weight models and lighter racing weight models.	**Weight** Lightest of all running shoes with the possible exception of track spikes. As with road shoes, you do get training weight models and lighter racing weight models.
Fit Not much different to a normal shoe fitting.	**Fit** Due to the stability required when crossing rough terrain the fell shoe has to fit closer to the foot. This means that they are a narrower and tighter fit than trail or road shoes. Often the runner has to buy a half size larger than their normal shoe fitting.

	Mountain Running	Fell/Hill Running	Mountain Marathons	Trail Running	LDWA Events	Long/Ultra Trail Running
Steep climbing	X	X	X			
Steep descending	X	X	X			
Contouring on steep terrain		X	X			
Periods of tarmac running				X	X	X
Hard packed trail normally with a loose surface such as gravel	X			X	X	X
Running across exposed sections of rock		X	X			
Mixed single-track path	X	X	X	X	X	X
Rough pasture/cultivated land such as fields		X		X	X	X
Steep loose rocky/stony surface such as scree		X	X			
Tall grassy tussocks/heather beds		X	X			
Steep grassy surfaces	X	X	X	X	X	X
Shallow/surface mud		X	X	X	X	X
Deep peat/boggy ground and mud		X	X			
Stream crossings		X	X	X	X	

All events may have elements of the different types of terrain. However, in most cases the bulk of the route would be run over the types of terrain shown above.

Shoe type Fell - Trail	Mountain Running F/T	Fell/Hill Running F	Mountain Marathons F	Trail Running T	LDWA Events F/T	Long/Ultra Trail Running T
F/T = will depend upon the nature of the route. It may contain elements that suit either shoe.						
Adidas	X	X	X	X	X	X
Asics				X	X	X
Brooks				X	X	X
Inov-8	X	X	X	X	X	X
Montrail				X	X	X
Mountain Bear	X	X	X			
New Balance	X	X	X	X	X	X
Nike				X	X	X
Puma				X	X	X
Salomon				X	X	X
Saucony				X	X	X
Walsh	X	X	X			

This list is not exhaustive and manufacturers are constantly releasing new shoe models that would fit into this list.

up wearing a soggy, sticky shirt. Being in the open as you will be on the trail or fell makes you more exposed to the effects of wind chill even from just a moderate breeze. At the best this can make a wet shirt an unpleasant experience, at the worst it has the potential for hypothermia.

Thermal vests
In winter most runners tend to wear the good old thermal vest and there are a large selection of them on the market. The vast bulk of them are suitable for the fell and trail runner. However be prepared to wear them outside the winter months.

Jacket.
Any distance runner should always take a jacket with them when training off-road no matter what the terrain or where they are running. You never know what might happen such as turning an ankle or just getting that tired that you fancy a walk. Having a jacket to put on to keep that bit warmer can literally be a life-saver. The jacket does not necessarily have to be waterproof, however, it should be windproof. Being wet doesn't kill but cold generated by the wind-chill can and does. Protection from the effects of the wind is much more important than keeping dry.
In some fell races the carrying of windproof jackets and bottoms is mandatory for safety reasons. Failure to comply will lead to disqualification or the runner not being allowed to start the event. Check the race requirements.

Shorts
The typical athletics short can be worn. However, if possible, it is advisable to use a pair made from a windproof material such as pertex.
A practise that is slowly gaining ground over here is the use of a longer style short. Known as a "trail short" the style has come across from the States. With a longer leg length and a number of useful pockets around them they are also often used in the adventure running scene. Whichever style you opt for is down to personal preference and what you, yourself, feel comfortable with. However, note the warning about lycra below. This also applies to shorts.

Bottoms
Wearing shorts in freezing cold conditions may look macho but can be counter-productive. Any uncovered skin is subject to exposure through low temperatures and/or wind chill. For the body to keep itself warm requires energy, the same energy that is used to power your running. Reducing the need for your body to fight the cold means that you have more energy to run with.
The preferred style of bottom is the trackster style made from man-made fibres. They are relatively light weight, move with your body and in wet conditions dry very easily. Always avoid cotton jogging bottoms, they are heavy and absorb water

very quickly making them even heavier and uncomfortable. Another material to avoid is lycra. One of the properties of this material is that it reflects body heat away from the body. This may be ok for the 100 metres track star but for the outdoor runner in possibly bad conditions this is the last thing they need. In these conditions body heat needs to be retained not reflected out. Re the section on jackets, with some events there is a requirement to carry windproof bottoms. Be aware that this does not mean normal running bottoms such as the trackster style. Rather it means more of the over-trouser similar to waterproofs. These can be bought separately or as a set with the jacket. There are a number of specialist lightweight models on the market now.

Socks.
A good pair of socks should not be underestimated. When running off-road there are a couple of factors that need to be considered that do not normally apply with road running.
Running off-road will inevitably result in wet feet either through running in

So what's the difference between windproof and waterproof ?

Waterproofs are as the name suggests designed to keep out water and keep you dry. High-tech waterproofs are made from a breathable membrane that allows sweat to wick away yet prevent water from entering. In reality they are very superior to low-tech waterproofs but even the best have problems coping with a sweaty runner. Low-tech waterproofs are just a basic waterproof shell. Water is kept out but unfortunately sweat is contained inside with the result that you can end up being just as wet as having no waterproof but you will be protected from the elements.

Waterproofs are also windproof.

Wind-proofs are not designed to keep you dry. Some are water-resistant and may keep a light shower off but in heavy rain you will get wet. However they are windproof and do keep the effect of the elements off you. Why is windproof more important than waterproof. Being wet does not kill you but being wet and cold does. In the outdoor environment the element that makes you cold, other than low temperatures, is the wind. The body generates it's own heat to keep warm, that heat is passed to the surface of the body where it provides an insulating layer. If the wind blows this layer away then that is when the body starts to cool down. Clothes provide some protection against this "wind-chill" but if the wind can still penetrate the clothing then it merely delays it rather than prevents it. Waterproofs and wind-proofs provide a windproof skin to retain the body's own heat. From the runner's point of view why wear wind-proofs instead of waterproofs.

Wind-proofs are generally lighter than water-proofs. They are also softer and more comfortable to wear. This means that the runner's freedom of movement is less restricted with windproof garments. They can also be worn in windy conditions when it is not raining.

mud or crossing puddles, streams etc. When feet are wet they are particularly prone to blistering. Any slight inadequacies in your sock or rough points on the inside of your shoe will be magnified and can cause soreness and blisters.

Another aspect of running off-road is climbing or descending steep slopes. If the shoe is not tight fitting, the foot can move backwards and forwards within the shoe. As well as causing friction, this can also result in the toes banging against the inside of the toe box of the shoe. In addition to blisters, this can also result in painful bruising to the foot.

A well-fitting pair of good socks will help prevent both of these problems. Try and get a pair that is quick-drying and will wick moisture away from your feet. Ensure that they are the correct size, the same as your shoe size. Sounds silly but I do know people who have worn the cheapest socks from the local market irrespective of whether they fit or not.

Ensure that there is no seam to rub against the skin. Some of the more quality socks now have padded comfort zones at the heel and the ball of the foot. This gives a bit more shock absorption from the impact of running.

One last tip. Try and get a dark-coloured sock. White socks don't stay white for long when you are an off-road runner. Mud and peat water can permanently stain light coloured socks and make you extremely unpopular with the person who does the washing in your household.

Hat

Approximately half of the body's heat is lost through the top of the head. In cold weather it is obviously advisable to wear a hat of some sort to keep the heat in. A hat is the single most important clothing item for maintaining body warmth. As with tee shirts, a hat made from one of the technical fabrics now available is preferable to the more traditional materials.

In the hotter, summer months a cap can help protect the wearer from the effects of strong sunlight. It can protect the scalp and eyes from the sun and as a result reduce the chances of overheating. In really hot weather, it can also reduce the chances of sunburn and sunstroke.

Gloves

Gloves keep the hands warm and in cold weather are an obvious necessity. We all have our own preference as to the type or material. One tip, at some point we all tend to wipe our nose on the back of the hand, it is more comfortable if the material is a soft one.

6.1.3 Rucksack or bumbag:

With the equipment and other effects that need to be carried, some form of bag needs to be used in which to carry them.

Most runners use what is called a bumbag. Basically this is a small bag that straps around the waist and rests on the runner's bum, hence the name. There are different styles of bumbag, the simplest being a single one-compartment tube bag with a zipper opening. The more complex can have separate compartments for luggage and drinks bottles, the bottle compartments may be angled to provide easier access to the bottles. A bumbag can be an effective way of carrying your event gear but is limited to 10 litres of space, anything over this and you can get irritating up and down movement due to instability of the bag.

Running with a bumbag shouldn't really cramp your style but if you have never done it before it may take a little getting used to. The basic rule is that the waist strap should not be that tight that it is uncomfortable but should be tight enough to prevent the bag from bouncing around on the waist. Some bags may also have additional straps to help secure the load in the bag. These are called compression straps and if

Two types of bumbag. The simplest on the right, is just a basic nylon tube that fits around the waist. The other on the left, is more sophisticated with a padded back support, central luggage compartment and two bottle carrying compartments. Note the compression straps for tightening up around the load and making it more secure.

your bag has them then use them. Having a bag bouncing around on your backside can be quite uncomfortable.

For heavier loads then a rucksack may be used. This rucksack may be combined with a plastic pouch (bladder) and drinking tube in order to make drinking on the run easier. These are sometimes known as hydration sacks.

If using a hydration sack then there is normally some form of luggage space within the sack that your equipment will fit into. There are many sacks on the market from small ones that you can only fit a bladder in, up to 30 litre Mountain Marathon sacks. These are all lightweight and very stable with waist and chest belt giving a snug individual fit. If using a sack, use it prior to the event in order to get used to it as you can get rubbing around the neck area which can be very annoying during the run and possibly causing skin-break and bleeding.

Pack your bumbag or sack to ensure maximum stability and also that there are no noises emanating from loose or clashing kit. Place soft clothing strategically to prevent hard objects rubbing against your back. During preparation, run carrying your chosen bum bag or rucksack to ensure you are comfortable with it, to the extent that you forget it is there.

6.1.4 Water carrying:

All runners know that when you run, you generate sweat which means that your body loses fluid. Maintaining a satisfactory fluid level helps maintain performance and that means drinking while on the run.

The importance of this cannot be overstated a 2% loss in body fluid can significantly impair performance possibly upto a 20% loss in running performance.

Unlike road runs, the majority of trail and fell races don't provide drinks at checkpoints. This is part of the character of running off-road and helps contribute to the wilderness/adventure challenge of these events. It is the runner's own responsibility to provide their own drinks en-route. The reasoning for this is two-fold.

> Things to be aware of .
>
> 1.It is generally accepted that drinking small amounts regularly is the better way to counter dehydration. Every 20 minutes or so is the norm.
> 2. Waiting until you are thirsty is too late, you are already dehydrated. Thirst is a very poor indicator of the body's need for fluid.

1.   Just the sheer logistics of carrying a drinks station out to a remote location. It is a lot easier and more eco-friendly for the individual runner to carry their own.

2. Look at the trail of discarded cups and rubbish leaving a feed station on a road race. Not something that you would want amongst natural unspoilt scenery.

On a five or six mile race, unless there is exceptional temperatures, the runner will probably get away with not carrying any fluids. However with any events of a longer distance then the runner will have to carry everything that they require.

Most runners carry a plastic bottle or two of their preferred drink either hand-held or in a bumbag. However, hydration sacks such as Camelbaks are starting to be used by more and more runners especially on longer distances. The bladder is easier to drink from regularly on the move but difficult fill up whereas the drink bottle is in effect the opposite.

It is common for the fell runner to drink from streams. In high mountain areas where contamination of the water is minimal, this may be relatively safe. However even on the higher ground there are still various water-borne parasites so think of using a water filter or purifying tablets.

> One of the main reasons for the deterioration in performance due to fluid loss is the loss of body salts that go with it. An electrolyte replacement drink containing salts and minerals is better than plain water, especially on the longer distances.

It is worth noting that on long and ultra trail races and also on LDWA events, there are usually feed stations situated around the course. This is because of the length of the route involved and the fact that the competitor can not be expected to carry all of the fluid required to complete the distance. However be aware that these feed stations will be located at the easiest possible site for them to be transported to and set-up. They will not necessarily be at equal distances around the course. As a result you may still need to carry drinks for those sections in-between feed stations.

6.1.5 Safety items:

Whistle.
In the unlikely circumstance that you do experience difficulties it would be handy to summon help. Some runners carry mobile phones but the reception in the wild places may not be that great. The more traditional and sometimes more effective method is by use of a whistle. See Safety Considerations Page 62: Summoning Help.

First aid kits
With some events especially LDWA and long/ultra trail or fell races the carrying of

a basic first aid kit may be compulsory. Even if you are just on a training run through a remote area it would be worth carrying one somewhere in your running group even more especially if you are running solo. After all accidents do happen. A relatively light weight basic first aid kit can be picked up for a few quid in most walker's shops. If you feel that it is still too heavy you could always discard some of the items that you feel that you would not need, just keeping the basics.

Survival bags

Again, as with the first aid kit, this will probably be compulsory on most LDWA and long /ultra fell and trail runs. Also worth considering carrying if running in remote areas ether alone or in a gang. The basic survival bag is a large orange coloured polythene sack. The theory behind it is that in the event of an accident the injured party is placed in the bag and the bag will help retain the body heat of the injured person until assistance arrives. The bag is coloured orange to be highly visible in the event of an emergency. Again they can be picked up for a couple of quid in outdoor shops.

Emergency food

Some events, particularly the long and ultra distance events, require the carrying of emergency food. This is not in case you get hungry but really in case of hypothermia either through weather conditions or enforced stillness through injury. Fighting the cold requires energy. Lack of energy can assist the onset of hypothermia. The emergency food is to provide additional energy stores in the event of something going wrong. With the competitive runner this may be just a simple thing such as carrying a Mars bar.

Others

In certain circumstances you may also want to think about midge repellent and sun cream. Vaseline or other cream for those chaffing area's. Especially for those events where you will be out for long periods of time.

6.1.6 Navigation aids:

Map and compass.

These are the two obvious navigation aids. In some events it may be compulsory to carry them especially on the longer events where the route may not be marked.

Do you know how to use them !

See our sister publication "Navigation for Off-Road Runners".

GPS

Still relatively new and as such there has been no rules devised about their use. However it is generally accepted that on those events where navigation skills are being tested such as mountain marathons and orienteering events then the rules for that event will ban them. Otherwise if an event does not mention the use of a GPS then in the absence of a ban it is considered acceptable to use them.

Altimeters

Nowadays altimeters can be built into sports watches and can prove to be a useful navigation tool. As above with the GPS, if the event rules do not specifically ban them then they are acceptable to use.

6.1.7 Required kit for events:

With some events there is requirement for the competitor to carry certain kit. This mandatory kit list is for safety reasons and is normally what the organiser judges is the minimum to help ensure the survival of the runner until the arrival of help in the unfortunate event of the runner having an accident. The carrying of the mandatory kit is taken very serious and breaches of it will mean that the runner will not be allowed to start the event. If the breach is discovered at the end of the race then it will lead to immediate disqualification. With fell running it may even lead to being banned from future events.

As a general guideline the following kit is the minimum for each of the different types of races. However all races are different and dependant upon the location of the run and the time of year, the organiser may list different equipment. Check the entry form and do a full kit check against the equipment list before you set off for the event.

Short trail races below 20 miles,

Not normally a requirement to carry kit. However it is always advisable to take waterproofs to the event in case of bad weather. Also be aware that you may have to carry your own drinks, and food/energy bars.

Fell races of any length.

The FRA recommends that runners take the following equipment to all races.
1. Windproof whole body cover (jacket and bottoms).
2. Other body cover that is appropriate for the expected weather
   conditions, for example thermal vest, leggings etc.
3. Map and compass suitable for navigating the course.
4. Whistle.

5. Emergency food (for long races).

These items must be carried in all category A long and medium length races. That means all category A events over six miles in length. With races of the other two categories B and C, the organiser may at his discretion, waive these requirements in fine weather. But even in fine weather it is still compulsory to carry them in AL and AM events.

Long and ultra trail races
With long and ultra trail races over 20 miles there is no mandatory kit list across all events. It is left to the individual race organiser to decide what is appropriate for his event. In this case, read the entry form closely to decide what you need. In most cases it may be similar to what is shown below for the LDWA events.

LWDA events
Again left to the individual organiser although in practice there seems to be a standard agreement on the following.

Minimum Summer Kit List.			
Trail or Fell Shoes.	Socks.	Shorts.	Technical Top.
Small Rucksack or Bum bag.	Food.	Drink.	Compass.
Whistle.	Watch.	Windproof Top.	Headtorch.
First Aid Kit.	Map.	Survival Bag.	

Minimum Winter Kit List.			
Trail or Fell Shoes	Socks.	Tights.	Thermal Top.
Small Rucksack.	Food.	Drink.	Compass.
Whistle.	Watch.	Waterproof Top.	Waterproof Bottoms.
Headtorch.	Spare Thermal Top.	Hat.	Gloves.
First Aid Kit.	Map.	Survival Bag.	

6.2 Safety considerations:

Safety has got to be on the mind of every runner whether you are just running round the block or running in the wild country of the Highlands. The safety of yourself and anybody that you are running with, first of all rests with yourself. Even on a relatively "safe" low level route, accidents and injuries can and do happen.

Speaking from personal experience, I know what its like to twist an ankle or pull a muscle and then have to walk three or four miles home. A friend of mine tore a calf muscle on a moorland run and had to be virtually carried two miles to a point where he could be picked up by car. So be aware of the possibility of such things happening and be prepared. However don't be put off by thinking that such things will happen to you if you go trail and fell running. The worst ever injury that I ever suffered was a broken ankle and I got that while slipping off a curb in a road race !

Below are a few wise words on safety. Most are common sense and, to be honest, should also apply even if you are only going for a run round the block.

6.2.1 Running alone.

In an organised event you always have the security of knowing that someone knows that you are out there and roughly where you are. On a training run you may be running on your own either on the moor, in the forest or on farmland. Accidents can and do happen and even on low lying farmland, in a worst case scenario, it may be hours before you are found.

Always tell someone where you are going and when you expect to be back. However, don't forget to tell them that you are back. Many an emergency callout has been caused by this !

6.2.2 Injury.

If a serious accident occurs that requires you to be immobile then stop and look for some shelter. If you are carrying one get into your survival bag. Ensure that you keep your body temperature up. You will quickly get chilled and cold once you stop running. If you are carrying one, use a whistle or mobile phone to summon help. If a third party is injured always try to ensure someone stays with the injured person but if circumstances dictate that you have to leave them to get help, ensure you have a the grid-reference of the injured person's location. If on an event, there may be a specific emergency telephone number to call. Use your first aid if you feel competent. If you do retire from an event *DO NOT* leave the competition area without advising the event centre. If the Mountain Rescue or other emergency services are called out after the event has finished you may be charged. Be prepared to give up your race to help fellow competitors, after all they may have to give up theirs to help you. *If in doubt over an injury then seek medical assistance.*

6.2.3 Carrying ID:

If anything does happen to you, one of the first things any rescuer will want to know is your name. It is always advisable to carry a small card with your name, address, contact number and details of any medical conditions on. This can then be laminated or just covered in sellotape to make it weatherproof. Keep it in your bumbag or elsewhere about your person. During a race, your race number leading to your entry form will provide details in the event of an accident. However in terms of medical information it will always be quicker if you are carrying it yourself. On training runs, especially when training alone, this becomes even more important.

6.2.4 Summoning help:

A large number of runners nowadays carry their mobile phone in the event of having to summon help. However it can be a false sense of security to rely on the mobile. There is no guarantee that you'll be able to get a signal in the remoter parts of this country and maybe even not some of the non-remote ones.

A cheap and reliable backup to the phone is to carry a small plastic whistle in your bumbag or somewhere on your person. This is standard practice among hill walkers and a very useful one to copy. It is surprising how far the sound of a small whistle can carry.

The international distress signal is six blows of a whistle, wait a minute and then repeat. Using a similar system of six flashes, a head torch can be used to signal in darkness.

Be aware that on some races the carrying of a whistle is compulsory as part of the required kit list.

6.2.5 Getting lost:

This can happen on both trail and fell runs even if the course is marked. A lapse in concentration and a route marker can easily be missed. However it is more likely to happen on unmarked courses or if training in unfamiliar areas.

The first signs of being lost will be when you realise that you haven't seen a fellow competitor for a while and/or the land features in front of you don't seem to match your map. Obviously the sooner you realise that you have a problem the easier it is to correct. If you are having doubts about your route then check, don't go blindly on. The worst thing that you can do is panic. Stay calm and appraise your situation. If necessary retrace your steps back to a point where you know you were on the correct route and continue your run from there.

6.2.6 Weather:

With both trail and fell running, weather conditions can have a large effect on both your comfort levels and your performance. Check weather reports prior to the event and when you arrive. Always carry sufficient kit with you to the event so that you are prepared if the need is to add or reduce your clothing.

If weather conditions are severe then it is the race organiser's responsibility to either cancel or change the event route to maintain the runner's safety. Under FRA rules and regulations, events crossing high level mountain routes are required to have a low level alternative route if weather conditions are considered too severe to use the planned route.

However be aware that in remote mountainous regions it is possible to get sudden, very localised, extreme changes in weather. These may affect all or part of a race route. One of the reasons for carrying mandatory equipment.

When you are tired on a long run you can very quickly become cold and unsteady. Just putting a jacket on to retain body heat can help a lot.

6.2.7 Appropriate footwear and clothing:

Wear appropriate footwear. Road shoes are not much use when running down a steep, slippery hill. Arriving at the bottom of a hill on your backside, or even worse, is not necessarily fun. Especially if it is a cow field !!

Dress appropriately for the weather conditions. In bad weather carry waterproof/ windproof clothing and be prepared to put it on. It may look macho only wearing a running vest in minus 10 temperatures but it doesn't do your reputation for sanity any good.

Wind chill is not often recognised as having a major effect on long term endurance, however, the more the body has to counter the effects of the wind the more energy is wasted. The correct clothing choice can have a great influence on countering wind chill. Take some alternative clothing with you to the event so that if the unexpected happens and the weather turns nasty you may have some extra layers to carry.

6.2.8 Obstacles:

Watch out when encountering such obstacles as styles and gates when you are tired. Lifting legs or moving in a different plane, can be a potential injury waiting to happen. Wooden boards and stone slabs can be very dangerous especially when wet making it easy to slip or fall.

Be Careful !

6.2.9 Fatigue:

Running off-road is more demanding in terms of energy consumption and fatigue can and will hit during an event or a training run. This is especially so on longer trail and fell runs. So do not be afraid to admit tiredness. Slow down or even stop – re-fuel and hydrate by eating and drinking. Knowing when fatigue has hit gives you a major chance of recovery.

Fatigue can take many forms but some indicative signs would be loss of communication, falling over and continuously wanting to rest.

If in doubt seek medical assistance.

6.2.10 Heatstroke and hypothermia:

Running in the open countryside does expose the runner to the more extremes of the temperature range. Obviously this will be affected by the part of the country that you are running in, how remote and wild the route is and the relative height of the route. Don't just assume that these only represent a danger in high level fell races. Trail races may also cross high level areas and even on low level routes the weather conditions may conspire against you.

Make yourself aware of the early signs of heatstroke and hypothermia. The person suffering from them is normally the last to be aware of their condition. Be aware of other runners around you too.

Heatstroke – some indicative signs are dizziness, headache, feeling hot.

Hypothermia – indicative signs are feeling cold, pale skin, lack of muscle co-ordination and being irrational.

If in doubt seek medical assistance.

6.2.11 Crossing streams:

In both trail and especially fell races, you may have to cross streams. This means that you get your feet wet. Now this all adds to the adventure of running the trails and I can't believe for one moment that you would really want to wimp out of the experience of paddling your little tootsies. However, in times of wet weather it will be a little imprudent to cross fast flowing water especially if it is deep.

Do not under-estimate the power of water. Even if only up to the level of your knees it can still have the power to sweep you clean off your feet. So use your common sense. As a general rule of thumb, do not enter water that looks as if it comes higher than half-way up your shins.

6.3 Meeting animals:

When running in the countryside, one of the things you'll come across is animals, whether it is wildlife or livestock. This may happen during training runs and races.

Dogs. You're likely to come across dogs on routes especially where the route runs close to town or villages. Taking your dog for a walk in the countryside is a popular pastime, I know I do it.

In the main, dogs don't give any problems to runners providing the runner gives the owner time to get the dog under control. Always announce your presence even if it is a simple "excuse me" and that goes especially if approaching the dog and owner from behind. The sudden appearance of a runner from behind can frighten both owner and dog and a frightened dog may respond by barking or even chasing. After all how does a dog know that a person running up from behind isn't a threat to itself or it's owner.

On the subject of dogs, if you are running with a dog keep it under close control and if necessary on a lead. This is especially so if running over the moors where you will probably meet sheep. Even if your dog ignores the sheep, just the presence of the dog can cause panic among them causing the sheep to run and possibly injure themselves.

Also it's always best to keep the dog on the lead when travelling over the moors between April and June. This is the nesting season for ground-nesting birds and dogs running in amongst the heather can seriously disturb the birds and lead to irate gamekeepers. And believe me, these are not a pretty sight.

Sheep. Not a problem. They tend to look at you as if you're weird and then just walk away.

Cattle. By law, any field that has a public right of way running through it and in which a bull is kept has to have a certain number of cows in the field in order to keep it company. The correct expression is to keep it knackered and docile. And it does work.

If going through a field with cattle in it, stick to the footpath. If the cattle are strung along the line of the path then just give them a wide berth and run around them. No one will shout at you for not sticking to the path. If you feel that it is necessary then slow down to a walk until you are past.

Don't get in-between a cow and it's calf. The maternal instinct may kick-in and it is possible that you could be seen as a threat to be chased off. Also never try to squeeze between a cow and a wall or fence. Although there may not be any intention to hurt they are big beasts and there is always the possibility of being accidentally crushed.

Horses. If you come across horses and riders, just follow the same rules as you would when you are in your car. Slow down and pass carefully without making any loud noises that may spook the horses.

Deer and other wildlife. Just enjoy the experience !!

Big Cats. There are lots of tales and stories of big cats such as pumas and panthers roaming the country. If you come across one of these the only advice is run like stink and hope that it doesn't like the smell of frightened runner ....

Safety tips

In fell races and those trail races that cross fell or mountain terrain, bad weather with poor visibility can present a serious risk to those runners who are not competent in navigation skills. If not competent in this area then either

1. Choose your races very carefully, or
2. Learn !

---

7. Route Finding, Waymarking and Navigation:

7.1 Waymarking and marking of courses:

Most short trail race routes are marked in some description or another. Markers may range from the big black arrows on a yellow background as seen in many road races, to red and white or other coloured tape down to white flour arrows laid on the ground. A lot depends upon the remoteness of the course. Markers have to be transported in and the bigger and more visible the sign, the harder it is to carry. The other side is that the larger and more visible the sign, the more obtrusive it looks in the landscape. The more remoter courses will therefore have smaller signs.

Irrespective of the size of the signs it is still the runners responsibility to ensure that they follow the correct route. Running with the head down with total concentration on the running and not being aware of what is around them can lead runners to make mistakes and stray off course. Even on a marked course the runner needs to be watchful for course indicators as not all junctions may be manned, just marked.

On the subject of marking, fell races can be a totally different kettle of fish to trail runs. Fell can be unmarked, marked or a combination of the two. Due to the remoteness of the courses, fell races are normally marked with the old red and white tape. Easy to put out and easy to take back. As a generalisation it's mainly just the short fell courses that are marked, the medium and long tend not to be. However that may depend upon which part of the country you are running in, for example, races in the North East are traditionally marked, those in the Lakes not. On the race entry form or other promotional material, it will tell you whether the course is marked. But be aware that this information will normally say "partially marked". This means that the course is marked but in the case of bad weather, visibility may be reduced to a few metres and so what may be easy to follow in good weather may all of a sudden become difficult to see. If the race form does not say that the race is marked then it is safer to assume that it is not.

Long and ultra trail races and LDWA events are not normally marked. Although those events that follow long distance paths, such as the West Highlands Way race, do have the path's own waymarkers to follow. The distances in these events normally preclude the organiser marking the course and so it is left to the competitor to navigate their own way round the route.

Be aware that even on unmarked courses there may be sections that are marked and in the race instructions, you will be asked to follow these markers. This is normally down to access and/or environmental issues where the organiser is required to ensure that the competitors follow a set course for a short distance. If this does occur then follow the instructions and keep to the markers. Access for future races may depend on it.

7.2 Navigation training:

If the course is not marked then there is an obvious requirement for the ability to find your own way round the route. The ability to navigate and read a map then becomes extremely useful. Even if the course is marked, bad weather or even just bad luck in straying off-course, can result in the runner having to find their own way.

Although not normally required for shorter trail races, with long and ultra trail, fell and LDWA events it is normally assumed that the competitor has the basic ability to navigate round the course if required. On most events the checkpoint locations and normally the route descriptions are known long before the event. This can allow the competitor to recce the route before race day and iron out any possible navigation difficulties. Something that is always recommended.

The skills of navigation are outside the scope of this book. For further information on navigation and map-reading see our sister publication, Navigation for Off-Road Runners.

Navigation skills can be very useful on some events. It pays to learn.

8. Participating in a Trail or Fell Run.

8.1 Pre-race:

Before leaving home do a kit check and ensure that you have everything that the organiser asks for as a minimum requirement. If a map is required ensure that you have the correct one and that it is up to date. You wouldn't be the first to turn up with a map of the wrong area.

Ensure you have safety pins with you. Not all trail and fell races issue them at registration.

Leave home to give yourself plenty of time to get to the event. Allow time to go through the registration process. This may involve queuing for your number, and kit checks. Also the parking area and toilets may be some distance away from the start.

8.2 Registration:

When you arrive at a trail or fell race the first thing to do is report to the race registration. The majority of trail and fell races do not issue race numbers prior to the event even if they do pre-race postal entry. They need to be picked up on the day. This is for safety reasons so that the race organisers know exactly how many runners actually start the race. The numbers of runners finishing the race will be checked and if there is a discrepancy between the numbers starting and finishing then the organiser knows that he has a problem and can take the necessary action. If you register for the race and pick up a number and then for whatever reason don't actually start the run, let the organiser know before you leave for home so that he can adjust his numbers accordingly.

At the registration, there may be an up to date weather forecast for the race area. Check this and confirm whether you need to change your clothing/kit choice.

Make sure you know where the start and finish of the event are. They may be some distance away from

Don't always expect race numbers at events. Those events that are organised from a predominantly athletics background such as a running club will use race numbers. As you pass through the checkpoint your number will be ticked-off a list of race numbers issued. Those events organised from a walker's background such as LDWA events and even some FRA events, don't tend to use race numbers but instead use a system of clip, electronic dibber or route cards. As you pass through the checkpoint the card is clipped, dibbed or marked in some way by the marshal as prove that you have passed through.

registration. In fact the finish may be in a different place to the start.

If you are unfamiliar with the course then it may be worthwhile recce'ing the last half mile or so in order that there are no hidden surprises waiting for you. This recce can be taken as part of your warm up.

Normally events will have a map of the course on display. Have a good look at it and see if you can identify any parts of the route that might give you problems. If you are going to be carrying a map of the course check it against the "official" map and mark it up especially checkpoint locations.

Both trail and fell races can be quite low-key and laid-back affairs especially at the start. Quite often before the start of the race, the organiser will give some last minute race instructions. Be prepared to listen and absorb.

8.3 Toilets:

Most road runners are used to having the convenience (excuse the pun !) of toilets close to the start of races. With trail and fell races this may not necessarily be the case. Because part of the attraction of these events is the "wilderness experience" then the start and finish may be some distance away from the nearest loo. In some events there may not even be one.

Most organisers do indicate on the entry form and in their race advertising whether toilet facilities are available or not and if not where the nearest are. As a general rule, the bigger the event and the less remote it is, then the more chance of there being a loo.

8.4 The event:

Take it easy from the start of the race. With most trail runs and virtually all fell races there is a hill close to the start. Be prepared for the sudden shock of climbing especially if you haven't done a sufficient warm-up. Once you are away, relax and enjoy. However be aware of where you are going and the ground that you are travelling over. This is one of the challenges of off-road running, unlike road running where you can put your head down and just plod round the course, with trail and fell you have to be constantly aware of where you are and what is around you. Even if in a marked route, a moments lack of concentration can lead to the runner straying off-course. Then there is the need for having to cope with challenging surface conditions. The joy of off-road running-having to think while you run.

Trail and fell races tend to be smaller events than corresponding road races. With smaller fields this may mean that there are periods during the race when you are running on your own. Be prepared for this and don't panic if it happens. However being on your own may mean that you have to concentrate that bit more to make sure that you don't miss any course markers and stray off the route. Follow your own race plan and pace. Don't run harder than you intend in order to keep up with a faster running group just because you feel the need for company. You will pay for it before the race is over.

On some events you do get what are called "crocodiles", strings of runners blindly following the runner in front on the assumption that he or she knows where they are going. Sometimes this tactic works, sometimes it doesn't and the whole string can stray off-course. If you are in a crocodile and you feel that they are heading in the wrong direction, then have the confidence in yourself and leave the group. You may end up at the finish line before them.

Virtually all trail and fell events have checkpoints spread throughout the length of the course. However, unlike road runs they are not there as a drink or feed station. Their purpose is to monitor the passage of the runners through the course and ensure that all are safely accounted for. As you pass through the checkpoint your number will be ticked-off a list of race numbers issued or if it is an event without numbers then your card will be clipped, dibbed or marked in some way by the marshal as prove that you passed through.

8.5 Post-race:

What happens after you cross the finish line ?

Unlike road races you don't tend to be handed a memento of the race although some trail races do hand-over tee shirts at the end.

The majority of LDWA and long/ultra trail races do have a meal after the finish. This may be a hot meal or sandwiches and a hot drink dependant upon event. The cost of this is usually included in the entry fee.

With short trail races and fell races the post-race celebrations are usually the camaraderie of hanging around similar minded runners and the craick in the pub afterwards. If you can, stay for the presentation. Trail and fell races are a lot more informal than other running disciplines and although the prizes aren't as grand as the other races they do sometimes get spread further down the field. On top of which a number of races do give spot-prizes and you never know your luck ....

I know that this has been mentioned before but with its importance, it can not be stressed too highly. With trail and fell races being held in the open countryside and the risk of runners getting lost, race organisers keep a check on the progress of runners. They know how many start the race and they know how many go over the finish line. If for any reason you retire from a race then you must report to the finish and ensure that the organisers know that you have returned. If you do not, then it will be assumed that you are missing out on the course and a search will be started. In the past this has resulted in call-outs of the emergency services only to find that the competitor is sat at home watching the telly.
Not very funny for the race organiser.

Above. Red and white tape on a marker cane. A common form of course marking in both trail and fell races. See Section 7 Waymarking of courses. Below. Whether trail or fell be prepared for a hill close to the start of a race and don't go off too fast at the start.

Due to the exposed nature of most trail and fell courses, the weather such as snow and rain, can have a dramatic effect on your comfort, running ability and safety. Make sure that you are aware what the weather forecast is and that you are adequately clothed.

9. Summary.

Running off-road is the most invigorating form of running that there is. It can stimulate the senses, the brain and the body. It can give you the buzz from exploring new-found country and terrain and the satisfaction of completing a physical challenge. However, it can also be one of the most intimidating especially for those not familiar or comfortable with the great outdoors.

The advice, instructions and knowledge contained in this booklet will go a long way towards taking you from the off-road novice to the experienced outdoor runner with the confidence and ability to face the challenges that you meet in your chosen events.

Enjoy ....

10. Appendices

10.1 Links.

At the time of going to press these details were correct but they may change over time.

Fell Runners Association – www.fellrunner.org.uk
Northern Ireland Mountain Running Association — www.nimra.org.uk
Scottish Hill Runner's Association — www.shr.uk.com
Welsh Fell Runner's Association — www.wfra.org.uk
Trail Runners Association – www.tra-uk.org
Long Distance Walkers Association – www.ldwa.org.uk
British Orienteering Federation — www.britishorienteering.org.uk

The author out practicing what he preaches on his local trails.

About the Author

Kev Shevels is a man who has forgotten more than most about off-road running. Its not that he knew it in the first place, its just that at his age the memory has started to go along with lots of other things such as a slim waistline ……………………..

A runner for over thirty years, Kev has been involved in off-road running for over twenty-eight of those years. During this time he has tried his hand at most of the different styles of this discipline, from fell, to trail, to mountain marathons, to ultra-trails, to orienteering, to mountain running. During this time he managed to raise himself up from being a lousy-level runner all the way to the dizzy heights of mediocrity. However, what he did also do is pick up an extensive knowledge and experience of running off-road which he has been able to pass onto others through coaching and encouragement.

A founder member of the Quakers Running Club and Durham Fell Runners, two of the most enthusiastic off-road running clubs in the North East, Kev has been a qualified UK Athletics Level 3 coach for the past nine years, specialising in Fell and Hill Running. Most of his coaching nowadays being done through Durham Fell Runners.

However, to some people his main claim to fame is as a race organiser. Over the last ten years, Kev has organised numerous races, from fell, to trail, to road and cross-country. Some years even organising as many as twenty events which partially explains the lack of training and the fact that he can no longer see his toes.

When not running, coaching or just promoting off-road running, Kev is an active member of his local mountain rescue team.

Acknowledgements

For encouragement, support and generally just putting up with me.

Lynne Shevels
Harry Manuel
Stu Ferguson

And all the runners that I've coached over the years.

The Run Off-Road Series

Run Off-Road is the name adopted by Trailguides for it's publications aimed at the fell, hill, trail and mountain runner. This series of books is designed to promote the sport of off-road running in all it's many forms and to encourage the participants to improve and develop their abilities and skills in order to further increase their enjoyment of the sport.

This is an evolving series of books that is constantly expanding. See our website at www.trailguides.co.uk and subscribe to our newsletter for regular updates on our range of publications.

At the time of writing the titles in the series include:

An Introduction to Trail and Fell Running
Downhill Techniques for Off-Road Runners
Uphill Techniques for Off-road Runners
Terrain Training for Off-road Runners
Mountain Marathon Preparation
Navigation for Off-Road Runners
Long and Ultra Distance Off-Road Running

Coming soon
The Mountain Marathon Book

Disclaimer

The information contained in these pages is provided in good faith, but no warranty is made for its accuracy. The contents are, at the time of writing and to the best of my knowledge, up-to-date and correct. However, the world is a changing environment and what is correct one day may not be so the next. The suggested training regimes contained in this publication are exactly that, suggested. It is the reader's responsibility to judge their own level of fitness and whether they are capable of performing any of the said activities.

No guarantee whatsoever is provided by the author and his team and no liability is accepted for any loss, damage or injury of any kind resulting from the use of these pages. Nor as a result of any defect or inaccuracy in them.

As with all outdoor activities, you and you alone are responsible for your safety and well being.